A CELEBRATION OF
200 Years

Union County, Kentucky, 1811–2011

THE
DONNING COMPANY
PUBLISHERS

The Donning Company Publishers

184 Business Park Drive, Suite 206

Virginia Beach, VA 23462

Steve Mull, *General Manager*

Barbara Buchanan, *Office Manager*

Heather L. Floyd, *Editor*

Stephanie Danko, *Graphic Designer*

Kathy Adams, *Imaging Artist*

Debbie Dowell, *Project Research Coordinator*

Tonya Washam, *Marketing Specialist*

Pamela Engelhard, *Marketing Advisor*

G. Bradley Martin, *Project Director*

Library of Congress Cataloging-in-Publication Data

A celebration of 200 years : Union County, Kentucky, 1811-2011.

     pages cm

   ISBN 978-1-57864-799-6 (hardcover : alk. paper)

1. Union County (Ky.)—Anniversaries. 2. Union County (Ky.)—History, Local. 3. Union County (Ky.)—Social life and customs. 4. Union County (Ky.)—Biography. I. Title: Celebration of two hundred years.

   F457.U5C45 2013

   976.9'885—dc23

                                       2013002502

Printed in the United States of America at Walsworth Publishing Company

TABLE OF CONTENTS

Jack Davis, a lifelong farmer and horseman who turned one hundred years old on January 4, 2011, saw many changes during his lifetime: machinery replacing horses, the women's suffrage and civil rights movements, the Great Depression, numerous wars, and the election of eighteen U.S. presidents. When asked what he thought was the secret to

his living to be one hundred, Mr. Davis said, "Family." He and his wife, Theresa, were blessed with eight children, twenty-eight grandchildren, and forty-one great-grandchildren, many still living in Union County.

Mr. Davis, educated at Morganfield High School, was a member of St. Ann's Church. During the 1961 Union County Sesquicentennial Beard Competition, Mr. Davis won first place for having the "Ugliest Beard," which was long and multi-colored.

Kim Humphrey of Union County First said that Mr. Davis was chosen as the Bicentennial Honorary Chairman because he represented so much of what Union County is about: farming and community leadership.

Jack Davis, a highly respected Union County native, died on February 19, 2012, at 101 years old.

Anniversary & Bicentennial Resolution

WHEREAS, Henderson Community College has been serving in Union County for 50 years;

WHEREAS, we desire as citizens to celebrate 200 years of existence for Union County, Kentucky;

WHEREAS, Union County pride, service and support are needed from each and every citizen in the upcoming year so that our celebration efforts shall be looked upon fondly by future generations;

WHEREAS, these Bicentennial events will give Union County an opportunity to share with those outside our county as to why Union County is a great place to live, work, start a business, and raise a family;

WHEREAS, we are taking time to celebrate what has made our communities in Union County great;

WHEREAS, we will celebrate our past, be grateful for our present, lay the groundwork for our future;

I, JODY L. JENKINS, UNION CO. JUDGE EXECUTIVE, hereby declare the entire year of 2011 to be a Bicentennial Celebration for Union County, and to be the _____200TH_____ anniversary of _____UNION COUNTY_____.

Jody L. Jenkins   _Jerry Manning_

Jody L. Jenkins, Union Co. Judge Executive   Jerry Manning, Bicennial Committee Chair

Signed, this __7__ day of __JAN_____, 2011

The Union County Bicentennial Committee would like to express its thanks and appreciation to everyone who helped make the Bicentennial Celebration a great success. From the ones who served on or helped the committees to the ones who attended the events, it was a year filled with many diverse activities with all events being well attended.

Special thanks to the *Sturgis News* and the *Union County Advocate* for their excellent coverage of the events and for their contributions to this book. Special thanks also to those who wrote narratives and provided photographs for this book: Bill Bauer, Barb Franks, Regina Catlett, Mike Guillerman, and others.

This book was made possible with assistance from the Morganfield Lions Club.

UNION COUNTY BICENTENNIAL BOARD

Jody Jenkins – Union County Judge Executive

Jerry Manning – Chair, Sesquicentennial

Joe Bell – Vice-Chair, American Legion/Sesquicentennial

Vicki O'Nan – Co-Director, Fiscal Court

Kim Humphrey – Co-Director, Union County First

Rev. Richard E. Pollard Sr. – Committee Member

Brian Humphrey, Travis Neitz, Bryce Danhauer, Megan Randolph, Jonathan Davis, Leicia Schneider – UC Leadership Class Members

Margaret Holt Chapman – DAR

Nyra Syers-Ford – Earle C. Clements Job Corps/MTC

Mike Moore – Morganfield Bicentennial Chairman

Sandy Arnold – Sturgis Chamber of Commerce

Joe Clements – Magistrate

Jerri Floyd – Magistrate

Joe Wells – Magistrate

Paul Monsour – UC Tourism

Carrie Dillard – *Union County Advocate*

Zelinda Fellows – UC Public Schools

Tommy Jenkins – Local Historian/Volunteer

Jim Dyer – UC Library

Cheryl Berry – UC Library

Debbie McClanahan – UC Library

Ty Rideout – Abba Promotions

Sean Sheffer – UC Planning

Jack Davis – Honorary Bicentennial Chair

Long before the coming of the white man with his states, counties, and towns—even before the red man and his villages—there lay a lush, verdant valley along a thirty-six-mile stretch of what would come to be called the Ohio River. This broad expanse of undulating land would become Union County, Kentucky, approximately 360 square miles of "God's Country."

Geologically, the outcrops of the county consist of an alternating sequence of sandstone and shale with sand, clay, and silt along the river floodplains all rich with coal, gas, and oil. The terrain is, in general, rolling to hilly, the lowlands confined to the bottoms along the rivers. The area as a whole is well drained, the Ohio and Tradewater rivers and their tributaries being factors in the natural watering and drainage system.

The first inhabitants were the Mound Builders, an agricultural people ancestral to the Indians. The chief evidence of their existence has been found in the numerous mounds they built for burial, religious rites, and other purposes, hence the name "Mound Builders." Upon their arrival they found cane growing in great abundance along the riverfront, furnishing a resort for flocks of pigeons, wild turkeys, geese, and ducks, as well as for deer, otter, mink, wolves, wildcats, raccoons, and opossums. They were the last permanent Indian residents, who left between 1650 and 1690. Two fairly important Indian trails crossed the area and temporary villages of Chickasaws, Choctaws, and Shawnee dotted the landscape at various times.

The organization of all Kentucky counties is identical, and closely modeled after the Virginia county plan, which in turn was set up with the English county as a model. Kentucky was established from part of Virginia and became the fifteenth state in 1792, and nine years later Union County was formed from a section of Henderson County.

Union County is representative of Western Kentucky counties. It is typical for its location on a large, navigable river and its devotion to agricultural pursuits. It shares a thriving coal-mining industry with several other counties in this section of the state.

Its history, except during the Civil War period and when floods or other natural disasters struck, has been uneventful. Its people have worked hard, enjoyed simple pleasures, and built their agrarian society without receiving, or seeking, fame or notoriety in the world outside. Because of Union County's adherence to the normal, its story may be a richer contribution to the whole body of knowledge of American folkways than if that story were a recital of spectacular events.

EARLY TOWNS AND VILLAGES

ARNOLD STATION

Until 1906, Arnold Station existed only as a settlement of a few farmhouses. In that year, the Morganfield & Atlanta Railroad came through, and since most of the right-of-way obtained was on the farm of Newton Arnold, the name Arnold Station was given to the community.

A railway depot was built, and Sam and Fred Arnold and Bain Holeman established a general merchandise business. They bought and sold poultry and served as agents in the sale of hay and grain shipped from this locality. However, Arnold Station prospered for only a few years, and business ceased to flourish long before the discontinuance of the railroad in 1940.

BORDLEY

Bordley, lying seven miles east of Sturgis near the Webster County line, was once an important trade center, but declined because the Illinois Central Railroad missed it by two miles. Many of its houses were moved intact to Pride, which was on the railroad. There is agreement that Bordley began as a post office near the present site but disagreement as to the year and source of the name. The town had a blacksmith shop, a gristmill, and a hotel. There was always one doctor there and sometimes as many as three. One store carried a stock of drugs in addition to other merchandise. Bordley enjoyed considerable prosperity until the War Between the States, when the predatory practices of both armies wrought such havoc that the merchants moved away and did not return until the conflict ended.

BOXVILLE

In 1858, Lincoln (Calvin) Agin moved into this area and set up as a shoemaker in a house of such size and shape that people derisively called it the "box" house. But success at his trade won him respect, and when in the 1850s Agin, along with David Springer, bought the first five acres for a contemplated town, it was thought fitting to name it "Boxville." Springer started a blacksmith shop, which was followed by a general store and numerous other businesses, and in 1870 Agin built a tobacco factory, long considered the finest in the county. In 1884, the Boxville Post Office was established. A large one-room schoolhouse was built and was the only place to hold religious services and other public activities so the Methodists, Baptists, and Christians all held services there.

CASEYVILLE

In the mid-1820s, when Peter and Samuel Casey were investigating the possibility of coal at Dekoven, Nicholas Casey landed his flatboat in a wilderness near the confluence of the Ohio and Tradewater rivers in southwestern Union County. He established a ferry and woodyard there, and presently boats bound up and down the river began to tie up at Casey's Landing for provisions. Casey's Landing became the town of Caseyville by action of the State Legislature in 1837, largely through the offices of Nicholas Casey, who was serving in the Assembly at the time. At one time Caseyville was credited with being the most prosperous community in Union County, having a hotel, three general stores, two drugstores, two grain dealers, a dealer in agricultural implements, a hardware store, two blacksmith shops, a grocery, two livery stables, three shoe shops, a wagon shop, an undertaker, a distillery, a butcher shop, a tobacco stemmery, a cooper shop, a harness shop, a flourmill, a barbershop, two millinery shops, a bank, a newspaper, and a number of beautiful residences. Successive disastrous floods, however, reduced the prosperous settlement to but a ghost of its former self.

COMMERCIAL POINT (BUFFALO CITY)

Commercial Point, near the outskirts of Sturgis, was originally an open space in the forest where the road from Morganfield to Marion crossed the road from Caseyville to Providence. This convergence provided the name of "Crossroads" as a rival to the name "Buffalo City," suggested because of the large numbers of buffalo that came here to lick the salt deposits. Situated on the Tradewater River (once rivaling the Green River in navigability), it was an important trading point before the War Between the States. In 1881, the town contained a flourmill, a saw and planing mill, and a tobacco factory, as well as a dry goods store, general store, two millinery shops, two saloons, a small jail, and a frame schoolhouse.

CULLEN

Cullen, on the old Bordley and Morganfield road, was once a trade center, but it diminished and was swallowed by surrounding farms. The school closed and the children attended school at Little Union. The hamlet sprang into existence during the Greenback agitation and bore at first the name of Weaver City, in honor of James B. Weaver, the Populist presidential candidate of 1880. Cullen, for a time the home of Union County poet Dr. Frank Rhea, never had a church, though its exceptional moral tone is mentioned in a county history (1886). It was a Prohibition precinct when most of the county was selling liquor.

DEKOVEN

Coal was King in Dekoven (spelled "Dekovan" in the 1880 Henderson-Union Counties Atlas) until 1924. For nearly a century, beginning with the first coal mine in 1843, through a succession of mining ventures each inheriting resources from its predecessor, King Coal not only built a prosperous town but also extended its influence to education and religion, erecting schools and churches. In 1885, a large freight depot had been completed and a passenger depot was being erected. Dekoven became a division of the Ohio Valley Railroad Company with offices there and the coal mines were booming. There were about sixty houses, post offices, a large drug and department store owned by the company, and privately owned stores and places of amusement, with a population of about 250. As successive mining companies took over, conditions bettered with the modernization and enlargement of all mine property. Up-to-date houses were built and old ones repaired.

Then came the downfall of Dekoven in April 1924. There were 300 men on the company's payroll, which amounted to $40,000 every two weeks, and tonnage per day averaged 1,600. A. J. Morehead, company president, informed the union delegation that the mine was no longer profitable. He announced that the mine would remain open for the town's welfare, if the men would only listen to reason. At the height of the tension one of the delegates cursed at the old man, whereupon Mr. Morehead cried, "Let the damn thing [the mine] fill up to the grass roots." No one believed he meant it, but he did. All mining activities ceased, equipment and property were sold, and the mine opening was sealed.

GRANGERTOWN

Grangertown is located a mile north of Sturgis on Highway 85. It took its name from Andrew Grainger, who came from England. In 1844, he arrived on the Tradewater River, where he built a home and shed for a grist and sawmill, which he and his brother William operated until it was destroyed by an explosion. In 1886, The Cumberland Coal Company opened a coal mine nearby—No. 1, or the old Wardlow Mine—and built a tram road for the transport of coal to river barges at Caseyville. Men who worked in the mines built homes along this road and, as most of the families were named Grainger, the new settlement became known as Graingertown, the spelling becoming simplified with the passing of the years.

GROVE CENTER

Like many another little towns, Grove Center sprang to life with the coming of the railroad, flourished until the railroad ceased to be a vital factor in prosperity, and then declined. With the advent of the railroad in 1886, there was much agitation in favor of calling the station "Hooper," since practically all the land it passed through in that vicinity was owned by Mrs. Nancy Stone Hooper, and other local Hoopers were numerous, wealthy, and influential. However, the opposition was too strong and the place was named Grove Center, because it was the center point between the two nearest towns: Gum Grove and Spring Grove.

HENSHAW

This small settlement was named for William Henshaw, a pioneer settler, one of the county's largest farmers, and the first postmaster when the post office was established in 1887. Shortly after the coming of the railroad, the town housed a mercantile business, a tile factory, a flourmill and grain elevator, and a livery stable. Two disastrous fires swept Henshaw: one in 1923, destroying the flourmill, warehouse, and four dwellings, and the other in 1936, when the old livery stable, the old tobacco factory then used for hay storage, two large grain elevators, the depot, and two large stock barns were consumed.

HERMAN (VALLEY)

Herman, on the Henderson and Sulphur Springs road, was first settled by Dr. Joseph Roberts, who built a three-room house on the site. The Roberts Farm was adjacent to the 680 acres of land owned by George Henry Cottingham. It was Cottingham who built the village of Herman Valley, sometime around 1888. He built eight dwellings, a store (with a public scale), a blacksmith shop, five large stock and tobacco barns, a tobacco factory, and an undertaking establishment. When a post office was established, it was called "Herman" in honor of Mr. Cottingham's eldest son, Herman Eugene, later a dentist in Morganfield.

HITESVILLE

The Virginia state government issued land grants within the territory comprising this district to two Revolutionary War officers for services in the war, but the land was then an unbounded forest. Although there was no settlement, many small squatters' cabins dotted the principal trails. Outlaws of the stripe of Samuel Mason and John A. Murrell made up many of the original inhabitants, but they were driven out by the pioneers. Among these first pioneers were the Hites (originally spelled "Huets"). Henry Hite established the first store in 1850, and his brother Peter had a brick kiln. A post office was established in 1855. Most of the settlers were migratory and little by little the town disappeared. Years later rebuilding began, and at one time there were a hundred inhabitants in the town, with a blacksmith shop, two gristmills, a shingle mill, two stone quarries, a schoolhouse, a photographer's gallery, a contracting carpenter, and a doctor.

LINDLE'S MILL

It was in 1864 that J. W. Lindle built a mill which had two burrs, one for meal, the other for flour. Just in back of the mill were the Mt. Pleasant Presbyterian Church and the Mt. Pleasant School, built on part of the church ground. A storeroom soon followed the mill, as did a blacksmith shop run by Jim Heady. Lindle also had a still. At that time there was no settlement at Sullivan. When the railroad came and made Sullivan, that town drew nearly all of Lindle's Mill into itself.

LITTLE UNION

Little Union is on Highway 56 about three miles southeast of Morganfield. A Baptist church was organized there in 1860 and six years later the structure was built. Douglas Alton operated the blacksmith shop and probably the gristmill. A general stock store was owned by T. S. Barker and Jim Grissom. The post office was established largely through the efforts of Frank Hass, but for whatever reason he called it Ula, and it remained so for several years.

MORGANFIELD

Revolutionary War General Daniel Morgan never set foot upon, nor laid eyes upon, the land that would bear his name. A space had been cleared around the large spring on the tract of land which had passed into the hands of Presley O'Bannon through his wife, who was the granddaughter of General Morgan. It was here that it was decided to establish a town. There are varying versions of how Morganfield was selected as the county seat, but the one with the most truth, no doubt, is that there were three places under consideration: Uniontown, Caseyville (the two largest towns in Union County), and Morganfield. A legislative committee was appointed to make the final decision. The men went to Morganfield first, and there Jeremiah Riddle entertained them and kept them so well supplied with liquor that they never left to see the other places, but went back and reported to the Legislature that Morganfield was the ideal place for the county seat.

OWLTOWN

In the 1830s there was a hamlet called Owltown. It was in the bottoms of Highland Creek, near the bridge on the old Henderson and Morganfield road which passes Hitesville. There were several dwellings, a blacksmith shop, and a small store. In the early 1930s, a flood of Highland Creek swept the last visible remains of Owltown away.

PRIDE

If ever a town was created by a railroad, Pride was that town. The railroad was an easy outlet for the products of the farms and for years continued to pour sustenance into the town, supporting, among other businesses, a general store with an associated millinery department, a hotel, and justifying the erection of a high school and a community building for all sorts of town gatherings. Then, in the late 1920s, trucks made their first appearance as a competitive threat to the railroad. With road improvement they were able to go directly to the farms for produce and thence to the market. Freight on the railroad decreased alarmingly and finally, on December 16, 1939, the last freight train made its forlorn run. The depot closed and the rails were removed in the summer of 1940.

RALEIGH

The fine farming land behind it and its location on the Ohio River combined to make Raleigh an important shipping point. From about 1840 to 1860, Raleigh shipped more grain than any other river center in Union County. Before there were voting places in Caseyville or Uniontown, election returns were sent out from Raleigh. The Articles of Incorporation, 1851, speak of the construction of streets and alleys and public buildings, the digging of wells, and the taxing of all shows and exhibitions. In its heyday Raleigh boasted three dry goods stores, one of them brick, three large warehouses, a hotel, and a wagon and blacksmith shop. Unfortunately, a curious lack of foresight placed Raleigh not back toward the hills but on the river. The caving in of the riverbank and seasonal floodwaters eventually destroyed Raleigh's shipping and drove its inhabitants away.

SPRING GROVE

Solomon Blue came to this district from Virginia in 1803 and bought several hundred acres of land. James Blue lived in what is now Spring Grove, the name being self-explanatory although the spring is now extinct. In 1861, James Stanfield, an Englishman, opened a coal mine there, and then a store was opened, followed by a blacksmith shop and a gristmill. A post office was established in 1880 with mail arriving daily, and Thomas Haun served as postmaster for many years to come. Such progress increased the activity and size of the town so that it was soon considered one of the important places in Union County until the railroad came through in 1886 and missed Spring Grove, going instead through Grove Center.

STURGIS

A new design was introduced into the pattern of town-building in Union County when Sturgis was founded in 1886. The river made Uniontown, and the needs of local government made Morganfield, but the railroad and coal—those twins of nineteenth-century industry—made Sturgis. In each of these towns, the motive of its founding was woven into the pattern of its development through the years.

Samuel P. Sturgis had purchased 600 acres of land in the area and after considerable negotiations, the Cumberland Iron and Land Company secured the options held by Mr. Sturgis. Colonel Giles, who became the company's resident manager, platted the town, and the streets were laid out and graded under his direction. Sturgis, according to one version, was named not for Samuel P. Sturgis, but for his sister, Alida Livingston Sturgis, who was the wife of Dr. Kelsey. It is said that Colonel Giles, who also named the town, wished to honor Mrs. Kelsey in this manner because she had been very kind to him at the time of his wife's death in Louisville.

UNIONTOWN

In 1839, the Kentucky Legislature granted a charter for both Francisburg, at the mouth of Highland Creek, and the adjoining town of Locust Port. A competition ensued, and tradition traces the establishment of Uniontown to a quarrel between William David of Locust Port and Isham Bridges of Francisburg. These two men were on the verge of settling their differences with a duel when a mutual friend intervened and settled the dispute without bloodshed. The 1839–1840 Kentucky General Assembly passed an act uniting the two towns, and because of the happy solution, the new town was called Uniontown.

Within the next twenty years, Uniontown became a river boomtown. Union County's first newspaper was established there in 1855, and the 1860 U.S. Census reported a population of 1,046, making it the largest town in the county. At the height of its glory, the town boasted five dry goods stores, six groceries, two hardware and tin stores, five drugstores, three grain warehouses, three tobacco stemmeries, a furniture store, a flourmill, three shoe shops, a brickyard, seven churches, four schools, a private bank, three secret societies, two millinery stores, three livery stables, two hotels, three saloons, three blacksmith and wagon shops, a merchant tailor, and a newspaper.

WAVERLY

Even before a hut had been built, this area was known as "The Crossroads" because the Henderson-Beaver Dam road crossed the Madisonville road there. When John and Arthur Donnelly came along the Madisonville Pike around 1815, they pitched their tent at the crossroads to peddle their wares, and later built a small cabin. During that time The Crossroads was known as "Donnelly's Store," and after the Donnellys moved on, it became known as "Paynesville" for Jack Payne, an early Maryland-born settler. The Big Spring tract of land, upon which the upper section of town was built, went on the market with Hugh McElroy as the agent, and he renamed it "Waverly" after his nephew, Waverly Greathouse.

At one time, Waverly contained a cabinet shop, two blacksmith and wagon shops, a flour and corn mill, a distillery, and two drugstores. As time went on, the center of town moved from The Crossroads to what was known as Main Street, and when the railroad came through in 1906, the residents moved the town toward the depot, where they could watch the trains go by.

EARLY AGRICULTURE AND INDUSTRY

The new settlers to Union County found a country well forested with a variety of trees and "strong" soil. The expansion of the farmed area of the county was typical of the processes of the time by which forest became agricultural land. Much of the labor was undertaken and accomplished with the crudest of tools. During this period, which extended into the mid-1830s, the farmer computed his gains not in dollars of net income, but in acres cleared, in added buildings and equipment, and especially in the increased number and market quality of livestock.

Early industrial development was dependent either upon agricultural development or the development of coal deposits that underlaid a major portion of the area. Lumbering and milling grew as a result of available timber from the clearing of the land. Another industry based directly upon grain production was that of distilling. Next to agriculture, coal was the chief industry, and it remains so.

The earliest school in Union County, a little log building, was opened in Morganfield in 1812–1813. Its students were taught by Aquilla Davis, who was also the postmaster. Following Davis, a man by the name of Boice taught school in a log cabin in another part of the town.

In those early years, schools in most towns were taught wherever a vacant building could be secured, and children often brought with them their own little chairs and tables. In many cases, these dwellings also served as churches. In 1840, Mr. and Mrs. Benedict Wathen deeded to the school trustees of Caseyville a brick building "to be used five days a week for school purposes and two days a week for religious services." The first school in Sturgis, in 1888, was a private subscription school, and Sturgis was also home to the Ohio Valley College. The first public school building in Uniontown was erected in 1895.

Parochial schools first made their appearance in 1820 with the founding of Little Nazareth, a girls' boarding school, by a colony of nuns from near Bardstown. The name was later changed to St. Vincent, and coeducational education was offered there. St. Agnes School, originally named St. Rose Academy, was established by the Sisters of Charity in 1872. The Sisters of Charity later founded St. Ann's School in Morganfield.

Not far behind the first settlers came the frontier church. Methodist circuit riders and Presbyterian and Baptist pastors began to preach the gospel in Union County soon after the first cabins were built. Religious services were first held in settlers' cabins, but in mild weather "cabin preaching" was supplemented by camp meetings. These camp meetings gave rise to the growth of different denominations in Union County, the first being a Baptist congregation in 1812, followed shortly thereafter by a Methodist congregation in 1815.

Before 1818 there were no more than a dozen Catholic families scattered throughout Union County. So few were the early Catholics that the small wooden chapel at St. Vincent Academy was the only structure for Catholic worship between Breckinridge County and the Mississippi River. Sacred Heart was then built (1826), followed by St. Ambrose (1834), St. Agnes (1859), St. Ann's (1878), and St. Peter's (1910).

Other early churches established were Cumberland Presbyterian (1833) and Christian (1838). The few Episcopalians attended services at the Baptist Church building in Uniontown.

EARLY TRANSPORTATION

In the early days, Union County's river towns bustled. Uniontown, Caseyville, Raleigh, Locust Port, and Commercial Point were visited by boats that did a thriving commercial business with farmers and merchants. So vital were the rivers that the development of land transportation was slow, and the railroad era was postponed until the 1880s by the success of river transportation.

In 1886, the opening of the Ohio Valley heralded the beginning of rail service throughout the area. Early in the 1900s, the Louisville & Nashville Railroad gave Union County its second railroad and, save for minor changes, the rail facilities of the county were complete. Direct mail connection with all trade areas previously served by the river had been established and new marketing areas opened up. In these same eventful years came the telegraph, the telephone, and rural mail delivery. In the 1910s and 1920s, the automobile arrived, and toward the end of this period, bus transportation extended the area's facility for travel.

HISTORY OF CAMP BRECKINRIDGE

Camp Breckinridge was situated in the extreme western part of Kentucky, twelve miles from the Ohio River. It was named in honor of John Cabell Breckinridge, one of Kentucky's outstanding statesmen of the nineteenth century. At age thirty-five, he became the youngest vice president in the history of the United States, presiding over the Senate with conspicuous impartiality. Ironically, a few years later he was caught in the Civil War turmoil and eventually distinguished himself as a Confederate general.

This entirely modern Army camp, designed primarily for infantry training, covered about fifty-six square miles (approximately 36,000 acres at a cost of approximately $3 million) of gently rolling brown clay terrain in Union, Webster, and Henderson counties formerly devoted to farming. Plans for the camp were developed in Washington, D.C. in August 1941, with the actual construction beginning the first part of 1942. Working on an around-the-clock schedule during the early months, all

prime contracts had been filled within five and a half months. The cost of the new facility was over $35,500,000.

On July 1, 1942, the camp was activated. Headquarters was established in the brick schoolhouse in Boxville, a community taken over by the government as part of the military reservation, until it could be relocated to one of the new administrative buildings.

Hundreds of cream-colored frame structures dotted the Kentucky countryside. The new Army base consisted of hospital facilities, barracks, mess halls, warehouses, office buildings, chapels, service clubs, theatres, recreation halls, post exchanges, a laundry facility, an incinerator, a cold storage plant, motor repair shops, a sewage disposal plant, fire stations, paved roads, and sidewalks. There were a total of 1,512 buildings. Over time, the Army base would be home for over 250,000 soldiers.

Notable persons trained at Camp Breckinridge were Senator Bob Dole, a Republican senator from Kansas, and Jackie Robinson, an outstanding baseball player.

In May 1943, a trainload of well-guarded German prisoners of war arrived at Camp Breckinridge, making it the first

Approximately 1,500 families were required to sell 35,684 acres of land to the federal government for the construction of Camp Breckinridge in 1942. Selling their land for considerably less than they thought it was worth, many of the landowners had as little as ten days to relocate their family members, household goods, farm equipment, livestock, etc. and possibly find a new form of income. Mineral rights described by one land agent as "a nuisance" were not considered in the appraisals. Given the word of the land agents authorized to appraise the land, many of the landowners believed they would return to farming once the war was over, and therefore did not seek justice in district court in Owensboro. Promises were made that they would have right of first refusal to repurchase their land for the price they were paid, less damages, once the government no longer needed it as an Army training facility.

Army base in the United States to house POWs. They were treated very well at Camp Breckinridge. In return, they performed many duties on the Army base and on nearby farms. Over 3,000 POWs would eventually be housed here until the camp's deactivation in 1946.

Camp Breckinridge had two USO facilities in Morganfield: one on the corner of Main and Spring streets and one on the corner of Chapman and O'Bannon streets. The latter building was eventually moved to West Geiger Street. Both buildings are still in use today by the City of Morganfield.

The murals on the walls of the Non-Commissioned Officers Club were painted by German POW Daniel Mayer. After having numerous owners since the deactivation of the camp, the Union County Fiscal Court purchased this building and converted it into a museum and arts center. The murals still adorn the walls and are probably the biggest drawing attraction to the museum.

Camp Breckinridge was deactivated in 1946. Between 1946 and 1954, the camp was activated and deactivated several times.

When Camp Breckinridge was declared surplus by the United States government in 1962, the bodies of the POWs that were buried in a cemetery on the Army base were relocated to Ft. Knox, Kentucky.

Today, Camp Breckinridge is occupied by the Earle C. Clements Job Corps Academy. Gone are most of the buildings built for use by the Army, as they were replaced by more modern buildings. What remains are the memories of a troubled time in the history of the United States and the part that Union County played in it. What remains are the stone walls that were the entrance to what was once Camp Breckinridge. What remains is the discontentment of the families displaced by the building of Camp Breckinridge and their not being given the opportunity to buy back their land. What remains are the murals painted by that POW soldier who died before he could return to his native country and his family.

Camp Breckinridge—a huge part Union County's history.

Union County was hit by one of the most devastating floods in its history in 2011. Floodwaters reached their third-highest level in one hundred years when the Ohio River, the Highland Creek, and the Tradewater River reached near-record flood levels. Although there was some concern for the Uniontown Levee, there were no problems.

Several roads in the county were closed due to high water, and all of the floodgates in Sturgis except one were put into action. Although it was difficult to get around in the county, overall the people understood the need for the closings and adhered to them.

In order for some children to go to school, they had to be boated from one side of the flood flow to the other. Countless numbers of volunteers helped with the flood effort

by filling sandbags, building walls, distributing water, moving furniture, donating trailers and storage spaces, and pumping water out of flooded areas.

Emergency shelters were opened in several places in the county.

As the floodwaters receded, several government agencies arrived in Union County to offer financial aid to those who suffered damage from the flooding.

As Union County prepared to celebrate two hundred years in the making in 2011, some of the biggest voices in Union County lent their support to the planned festivities, collection of photos and memorabilia, and community involvement being generated ahead of the Bicentennial Celebration. They looked at the Bicentennial as a way to commemorate Union County's founding, educate its citizens about the county's history, and share Union County pride with the rest of the nation.

Savor the excitement of the Bicentennial, and carry the momentum of the occasion into Union County's next two hundred years! It is never too late to be a part of history.

"UNION COUNTY CELEBRATES TWO CENTURIES OF CULTURE & HISTORY"

by Jerry Manning, Chair, Bicentennial Committee

Union County is proud to celebrate its two-hundred-year existence in a Bicentennial Celebration that will take place throughout 2011!

Now is the time to get involved and take part in this significant milestone celebration.

Your Union County pride, service, and support are vitally needed to make this the biggest series of events in our history that will be recorded and looked upon fondly by future generations.

"WHY IS THE BICENTENNIAL IMPORTANT?"

by Joe Bell, Vice Chair, Bicentennial Committee/American Legion

The celebration activities and information will not just be for us living and working within the county. The Bicentennial events will give Union County a regional forum in which to tell our story. This is our opportunity to share our Union County perspective to others outside our county lines as to why UC is a great place to live, work, start a business, or raise a family.

We are taking this time to celebrate what has made our communities in Union County great, and also look forward and dare to dream of the next two hundred years—to begin to lay those foundations for the next generation. The celebration will be when the past meets the present and lays the groundwork for the future.

"WHAT IS OUR STORY?"

by Vicki O'Nan, Co-Director, Fiscal Court

Built on strong traditions of farming and coal mining families, our gorgeous county is set in serene countryside that features fairs, festivals, and rallies but also offers beautiful parks, recreation areas, golf courses, lakes, a museum, and a nature preserve. Union County is home to many companies, organizations, and industries in agriculture, healthcare, energy, and technology, some of which provide goods and services nationwide.

That is the point of our celebration—anything can be achieved in Union County, Kentucky! The world is our oyster! Union County provides a low-cost and friendly atmosphere in which to do business, to enrich our children with a great education, and to administer excellent access to healthcare for our citizens.

"CITY OF MORGANFIELD ALSO CELEBRATES BICENTENNIAL"

by Mike Moore, Chair, Morganfield Bicentennial Committee

In 1811, in a field that was part of Daniel Morgan's land grant, a new city was founded. The plat for the city of Morganfield was made by James Townsend, consisting of 103 lots, six streets, and two alleys. Two hundred years later, Morganfield partnered with Union County in celebrating our Bicentennial with events that highlight our county and our city. Join us in that celebration.

"WHO WILL WE REACH?"

by Kim Humphrey, Co-Director, Union County First

This is a time to make those new to our community feel welcome and to become engaged in our history and be a part of developing our future.

We will provide a regional forum and showcase the unique features of doing business, retiring, or raising a family within Union County.

We invite those who have moved away to return, celebrate their roots, and go out into the world and further share our story. This is your time to help your community continue to flourish into the next two centuries and sell others on the benefits of locating within Union County. Learn more about how you and your business can get involved in the Bicentennial!

Breakfast KICKOFF

January 7, 2011

More than fifty people from throughout Union County gathered at Peak Brothers BBQ in Waverly to attend the Kickoff Breakfast for the Union County Bicentennial Celebration. Jerry Manning, chair of the Union County Bicentennial Board, welcomed everyone. Joe Clements, magistrate of District 5, made welcoming remarks as well. The Blessing of the County was offered by Father Freddie Byrd, pastor of St. Peter's and Sacred Heart Catholic Churches: "Thank you for the many blessings we have received and we pray that You continue to bless this County and the people who live here."

Union County Judge Executive Jody Jenkins proclaimed the entire year of 2011 as the official Bicentennial of Union County. Various events for the year's 2011 Bicentennial Celebration were shared with anticipation. These events were held throughout the year and are presented on the following pages.

ABRAHAM LINCOLN AND FREDERICK DOUGLASS COME TO TOWN

Abraham Lincoln, the sixteenth president of the United States, returned to Morganfield on this cold, snowy day in February. He was last here in 1840 when he stumped for William Henry Harrison, the presidential candidate for the Whig Party. Also here on this day was Frederick Douglass, the grandfather of the civil rights movement.

Mr. Lincoln and Mr. Douglass met to discuss the right of African American soldiers to equal pay, equal supplies, and equal commendations during the Civil War. They also discussed the poor treatment of black soldiers who were taken prisoner by the Confederate Army. The soldiers were usually tortured and then executed.

At the end of the meeting, Mr. Lincoln agreed to eventually secure equality for all soldiers fighting for the United States. The Civil War claimed over 40,000 black soldiers and hundreds of thousands of white men from the North and South. At the conclusion of the Civil War, Mr. Douglass said: "When the War ended the lion gates of bondage swung open and just like Jericho, the walls came tumbling down." This meeting of the two great minds would go down in history as the Lincoln–Douglass Debate.

At the conclusion of Lincoln and Douglass' meeting, the Boy Scouts and children from the Union County Public

Library Children's Program recited the Gettysburg Address followed by a stunning rendition of "God Bless America" by Mrs. Willie Wilson.

Abraham Lincoln was portrayed by Jim Sayre of Lawrenceburg, Kentucky, and Frederick Douglass was portrayed by Michael Crutcher, a native of Union County.

This Bicentennial Celebration event was sponsored by the City of Morganfield.

Lincoln's Speech

The biggest event of 1840, an election year, was a political speech by Abraham Lincoln; the only political speech, it is said, that he ever delivered in Kentucky. General William Henry Harrison and John Tyler were the Whig candidates for president and vice president, and Union County during this campaign was largely Whig. Therefore, when word reached Morganfield that a stump speaker of that persuasion, Abraham Lincoln by name, was to hold forth at Shawneetown, Illinois, a short distance down the river, a delegation was sent to the rally to secure his oratorical services. The best-remembered incident of the day concerns the cannon which was brought along to fire a salute. It was set fast against a tree, and since no provision was made for the rebound, the cannon was literally blown to pieces.

Morganfield was also visited later in the 1840s, not by a future president of the United States, but by a former president. After serving out the term of Harrison, John Tyler turned to his property affairs. Among these was a debt against a Virginian who had inherited from his father a Revolutionary War land grant in the lower part of Union County. Tyler accepted this land for the debt and, in the summer of 1846, came to Union County to see the tract and to straighten out a disputed boundary.

Abraham Lincoln and Frederick Douglass took a few minutes before their famous debate in the courtroom of the Union County Courthouse to sample pieces of cherry pie. After having enjoyed each of the pies, they chose Heather Kirton's cherry pie as the best. This Bicentennial Celebration event was sponsored by Old National Bank.

BEARD CONTEST

Before Abraham Lincoln and Frederick Douglass left the courtroom for the Strawberry Tea Social, they consented to be judges for the Beard Contest. Of the five entrants, Mr. Lincoln and Mr. Douglass chose Bill Johnson for the longest beard, Clint Nalley for the thickest beard, and Lee Baird for the best overall beard.

This Bicentennial Celebration event was sponsored by Doby's Barber Shop.

The Union County Public Library hosted a Strawberry Tea Social at its Morganfield Library following the Lincoln and Douglass Debate. A variety of cookies along with chocolate-covered strawberries and punch were served by several students of the Earle C. Clements Job Corps Academy's culinary arts class to the large group in attendance. Special guests at the Social were Mr. Lincoln and Mr. Douglass, and those attending enjoyed talking with them.

Abraham Lincoln's only political speech in Kentucky was in Morganfield in 1840. In honor of this event, a cannon was brought along to fire a salute to Mr. Lincoln, who was stumping in Union County for "Old Tippecanoe," William Henry Harrison, the Whig Party presidential candidate. It had been set against a tree. Since no provision had been made for the rebound, when it was fired, the cannon literally blew apart.

The breech of this dismantled cannon was used for a long time as a doorstop in the James G. Taylor Store in Morganfield. When Lincoln authority and collector Dr. Louis A. Warren of Ft. Wayne, Indiana, visited Morganfield about 1921, it was given to him. The breech eventually made its way to the Lincoln Memorial Home at Hodgenville, Kentucky. It is now in the museum of the Kentucky State Historical Society in Frankfort, Kentucky. The barrel of this cannon served as a corner marker on the G. D. Robertson Farm near Morganfield until about 1922, when it was stolen.

On this day of the Bicentennial Celebration, Abraham Lincoln and Frederick Douglass unveiled that cannon breech, which was on display at the Union County Public Library during the Bicentennial Celebration.

LUNCH AND BIRTHDAY PARTY AT BRECKINRIDGE PLACE

Mr. Lincoln and Mr. Douglass were honored guests for lunch and a birthday party with the residents and their families of Breckinridge Place. The Union County Homemakers provided the dessert.

This Bicentennial Celebration event was sponsored by Eidetik, owners of Breckinridge Place.

A nice crowd was in attendance at the Bicentennial Fashion Show held at the Camp Breckinridge Museum and Arts Center. "We have acquired an extensive costume collection during our eighteen years of bringing live theatre performances to Union County," said Judy Holiday, chairman of the Unicorn Players. "Since fashion is a reflection of world events, this is also a history lesson, hopefully an entertaining one." Not only did those attending the Fashion Show enjoy fashions from the 1800s to the present, they also enjoyed a lovely luncheon.

This Bicentennial Celebration event was sponsored by the Union County Unicorn Players.

Show QUILT

More than 125 quilts with features ranging from monsters to classic white-on-white candlewick were on display at the Camp Breckinridge Museum and Arts Center for this year's Quilt Show. Visitors were able to see the different designs and techniques used for the quilts and vote in the different categories for what they liked best. A highlight of the show was the display of the "Kentucky Counts! 2010 Census Quilt" that was made of 120 squares featuring the diversity and creativity of the Commonwealth. Union County's square was made by Mary Rose Thomas and represents Union County's commitment to agriculture, youth, and conservation.

Visitors were given the opportunity to see where the Union County Quilt Trail signs are painted.

Entertainment for the weekend featured the Wildwood Flowers Dulcimers from Henderson County. Their music ranged from classic gospel music to Irish tunes. Five Mile Curve from Booneville, Indiana, entertained with bluegrass music.

Vendors selling fabrics and notions set up for business. Refreshments were available for purchase.

This Bicentennial Celebration event was sponsored by the Camp Breckinridge Museum and Arts Center.

Several hundred visitors attended this event, which was held at the Uniontown City Park. Civil War reenactors from Kentucky, Missouri, and Indiana provided visitors with history lessons and entertainment. Cannons were fired, children were able to shoot long guns and play with "spinners," memorabilia was displayed, and music and reenactments were enjoyed by all. Special music was provided by Mike Lawing.

Mrs. Betty Phillips, portrayed by Pam Rowley of Morganfield, presented a replica of the 4th Regiment flag of the Kentucky Confederate Infantry at Camp Boone, Kentucky, to Uniontown Mayor Ricky Millikan, who then took part in the flag-raising ceremony.

Mrs. Phillips, a native of Uniontown, followed her husband into the 4th Regiment. While he fought in the battle, she tended to the wounded soldiers and procured food, clothing, and other items when they were

needed. She sewed garments for the soldiers in the Regiment and was highly regarded by her husband's colleagues.

In Glasgow, Mrs. Phillips appeared before a Federal commander to secure a way back to Uniontown, but was arrested as a Confederate spy and imprisoned. When the war ended, she had in her possession the battle flag that was at the Adam Johnson Camp of Confederate Veterans. When the camp closed, the veterans who remained gave the flag to the United Daughters of the Confederacy. It is now on display in the Confederate Historical Room in the Old Capitol Building in Frankfort.

Mrs. Phillips and her husband, Captain William Phillips, are buried in the Uniontown City Cemetery.

This Bicentennial Celebration event was sponsored by Consolidated Grain and Barge, Floyd's Market, Uniontown Food Mart, Jim David Meats, and Lee Nally.

The War Between the States

Union County, like most of Kentucky, was a "house divided against itself" during the War Between the States. Fighting in Union County consisted chiefly of skirmishes, and these were numerous. The summer of 1864 was the most eventful period during the course of the war for the county. Operations, largely of an offensive nature, by Confederate General Adam R. Johnson brought Federal forces under Lieutenant Colonel S. F. Johnson and General J. M. Shackelford into action. Two of the most important engagements within the county took place during this period. One was at Geiger's Lake, where a minor battle was fought, and another was at Uniontown, where a running fight led to quick capitulation by the Federal troops.

Tournament

Avid golfers gathered at the Elkwood Golf Course in Sturgis to enjoy a game of golf and some good competition among themselves. Those who placed in the top three categories won cash prizes.

Show CAR AND TRUCK

June 4, 2011

Visitors to the Car and Truck Show at the Sturgis City Park got a chance to return to a bygone era when they were treated to an outstanding array of over eighty classic cars and trucks from classics like the 1934 Chevrolet to souped-up models. Individuals competing for prizes entered about fifty cars and trucks. The Evansville Road Knights brought their vehicles but didn't compete for prizes.

The stars of the show were Sam Jones and Dale Moody with the car that won the 1962 points championship at the Sturgis Drag Strip.

This Bicentennial Celebration event was sponsored by the Sturgis Kiwanis Club, Dodge Hill Mining Company, Sturgis Antique Mall, Alan's Body Shop, and Thornsberry Insurance. The City of Sturgis provided the use of the Sturgis City Park.

GET FIT KENTUCKY TRIATHLON AND DUATHLON

Over 150 athletes participated in the annual Get Fit Kentucky Triathlon and Duathlon held at Moffit Lake. On a day with high humidity and temperatures, the athletes swam, ran, and biked. All participants received T-shirts, a free lunch, and many other items that were donated by local businesses.

The overall winner in the men's triathlon was Matthew Bartsch and Laurel Jacobs won in the ladies' triathlon. The overall winner in the men's duathlon was Mike Dimmerly and Jessica Carder won in the ladies' duathlon.

This Bicentennial Celebration event was sponsored by the Union County Get Fit Kentucky organization.

Fans of traditional and contemporary country and bluegrass music enjoyed two concerts at the Sturgis Amphitheater. The Friday night performers were Kentucky Opry Stars of Tomorrow Carson and Hunter Wright and Savanna Gardner. Donations from this concert benefited the Sturgis Youth Center.

Todd Cowan and the Sodbusters, a bluegrass quartet, entertained on Saturday night. Donations from this concert benefited the Sturgis Chamber of Commerce.

The sixty-second Union County Fair was a week packed with games, rides, competitions, exhibits, and contests.

Winners of the different contests were:

Miss Teen Union County Fair: Courtney House

Miss Preteen Union County Fair: Bailey Barnes

Miss Union County Fair: Amanda Gough

Little Miss and Mister Union County Fair:

Reese Sprague and Weston Farmer

Baby Contest: Paisley Landsdowne, Zeke

Bates, Raelyn Gamboa, Jaxton Hansboro,

Paxton Morgan, and Thomas Day

Other competitions were the Union County Newlywed and Not-So-Newlywed Games, lawn mower derby, demolition derby, pedal tractor pull for kids, horse show and rodeo, carnival rides, food and games booths, goat show, adult tractor pull, and Union County 4-H Horse Drill Team.

Union County Bicentennial Honorary Chairman Jack Davis, one-hundred-year-old lifelong horseman and Union County fairgoer, was in attendance at the fair.

Picnic FOURTH OF JULY

The Fourth of July Community Picnic was scheduled to be on the lawn outside the American Legion Building in Morganfield, but because of the weather, it was moved inside. It certainly didn't dampen the spirits of those attending. Bingo was played by everyone for cash prizes and a crafts table was set up for the children. The Key Club prepared food and drinks for those in attendance. Music entertainment was performed by Davis Schnerr from Newburgh, Indiana. He played a variety of patriotic songs and easy listening music.

This Bicentennial Celebration event was sponsored by the Bicentennial Committee.

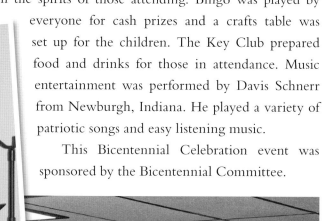

ANDERSON FARMS

155 YEARS AND GOING STRONG

Let it be recognized and celebrated that the family of William Stephen Anderson has owned and operated a Union County farm since 1856.

The present Steve Anderson Farms operation began in 1856, when Green Robinson began farming what is now known as the Robinson Farm located on Tina Waggener Road, west of Morganfield. Green Robinson was the father of Nora Agnes Robinson, wife of John Nathan Anderson. John Anderson purchased the present Anderson Farm, west of Morganfield near Highway 56, in 1904. He built his home in 1910, and it is still in use by Steve and Callie Anderson.

The original log cabin stands in the yard and is now a guesthouse, personal museum, and office of the farming operation. A deerskin-covered family Bible records the lives, deaths, and marriages of all the Andersons in Union County.

The farmhouse was built in 1910, complete with a pit to generate carbide gas for the lights inside. The Anderson house was altered according to the needs and finances of the family living in it. Rooms were added one or two at a time, sometimes with complete changes of purpose.

Following the death of Green Robinson in 1908, John Anderson began farming the Robinson land as well as his own until his death in 1944. John's two sons, William Allen "Bill" Anderson and John Nathan "Nace" Anderson, then continued the family farm operation.

Since the late 1960s, Bill's son, William Stephen Anderson, has owned and operated Steve Anderson Farms. More cropland has been added through the years in Union County, as well as Henderson and Webster counties.

144 YEARS

By 1867, James S. Pride and all of his children, some married, moved to Union County, Kentucky. He leased fourteen acres of land from Daniel B. Hammack for eight years. Included in the lease was the statement, "and if he lives, two years rent free, extra 10 acres for his use, said Pride, to clear fences and cultivate the land twice for its use." He lived until 1886 and had five more children. James S. Pride was buried in 1886 in a cemetery in Bordley.

Ronnie Paris is the fifth generation to farm in the Pride area. His acreage and machinery have expanded. He lives in a beautiful home on the Pride countryside that once belonged to his parents, Monie and Ryvers Paris, who had three children: Bobby Jo, Myra Lee, and Ronnie.

There is a famous book and mystery associated with Ronnie's ancestors. Ronnie's great-great-grandmother was Piety. Her father was David Thompson Porter. He was one of the

many witnesses to the Bell Witch escapades. David's sister, Rebecca, was the best friend of Betsy Bell.

In the year of 1804, John Bell wanted to provide a better life for his family. The farmer discovered an opportunity in Robertson County, which is located in Tennessee. The land that they moved onto was approximately 320 acres. The soil was fertile and perfect for growing crops and rested along the famous Red River. Toward the end of the summer in the year 1817, the peaceful life that the Bell family had grown accustomed to would quickly change forever. It is believed that the Bell Witch came to the home with the intent and purpose of killing John Bell. She also seemed interested in preventing his daughter, Betsy, from marrying a young man that she had taken interest in.

1873

This farm has been in continuous ownership and cultivation since the first tract was purchased on October 21, 1873. Since its purchase, this land has always been farmed by descendants of William Lewis Smith.

Tract 1, consisting of fifty acres, was purchased by William Smith from Wm. R. Tate and Louisa Tate for $1,000 in 1873. Mr. Tate was the brother of Mary E. Tate, the wife of Hiram H. Smith. Their daughter, Harriett Truman Smith Nall, was the maternal grandmother of the children of Benjamin Lewis Smith, who still own the farm.

Tract 2, consisting of forty-five acres, was purchased by William Lewis Smith in 1885 from Samuel Holeman Sr. and Malvina for $900.

Tract 3, consisting of fifty acres, was purchased in 1895 by William Smith and his son George William Smith from W. W. Pierson and Sue for $2,025.

Tract 4 was purchased in 1934 by Benjamin Lewis Smith and George Byron Smith and their wives from G. W. Holt and Lizzie.

Tract 5 was purchased by Benjamin Lewis Smith and Lillian from George Byron Smith and wife Eva. This was part of a larger purchase by George Byron from the Ed O'Nan estate.

The cost was about $285 per acre.

Sam Lewis Smith's father, Benjamin, said that the old log barn that stood for many years near the highway was a mule barn. The mules stayed there during the crop-growing season. In the off-season they were brought back to the homeplace. There was a well for watering the stock. It was only closed a few years ago. Sam's grandfather built a new house in the early 1900s with lumber cut on the farm and milled at Ed O'Nan's sawmill. The logs and lumber were moved by oxen. That house was removed in 2007. The current owners of these tracts that make up the farm are children of Benjamin and Lillian Smith.

In the 1900s, a drainage ditch was dug by machine going to Cypress Creek. This ditch, known as the Smith ditch, literally made the area the rich farming land that it is today. With the installation of field tile and smaller ditches, folks speak of the Pond Fork area as having some of the better farmland in the county. Previously all excess water had to drain over to Webster County to get to the Tradewater River. Grandfather George William Smith went with another fellow farmer obtaining right of way to dig this ditch. The machine was shipped to Sturgis via railroad in pieces from Iowa and was sent back after the job was finished.

In December 1854, Springer Morgan and his brother Elias Morgan purchased property in Union County from the estate of Major William Winston consisting of 303 acres at $6.77 per acre. In May 1856, Springer moved to Union County from Jefferson County and built his two-story home, probably around 1858. In 1875, Springer took sole possession of the property in Union County by trading property he owned in Jefferson County for his brother's half. Springer's daughter, Elizabeth "Bettie" Morgan, married William Edward Hamner of Morganfield. The farm was deeded to Bettie and William Hamner. The home and farm subsequently passed from them to their only daughter, Annie Hamner Meacham,

the mother of William Tandy Meacham. The property was then deeded to William Tandy and Jane Dudley Meacham in the 1960s. William and Jane had made it their home since 1948. Upon the death of William Meacham in 2008, part of the farm (forty-plus acres) and the home were deeded to Ralph and Evelyn Meacham and the remainder of the farm to William and Jane's other three children: Margaret Shirel, Rodman Meacham, and William E. Meacham.

Corn, soybeans, Shorthorn cattle, hogs, and horses have been produced on the farm with great pride by the heirs of Springer Morgan. Most of the farm is now rented for the production of corn and soybeans. Ralph and Evelyn Meacham are raising quarter horses and hay on their portion.

The two-story log structure originally consisted of four large rooms and a hallway both upstairs and down. We believe that the house was constructed around 1858 because one of the hinges on an interior door has "1858" stamped into the metal. The hinge is unique in that it was not put together with a pin, but fits together much like a ball-and-socket joint. The kitchen was a separate one-story log structure. Many of the logs are eighteen to twenty inches across. When Springer Morgan built the house it was immediately covered with weather boarding, as the logs have never been exposed to weather. We

discovered this when replacing the siding a couple of years ago. In 2009, a hailstorm damaged the aluminum siding, so it was removed, and the original weather boarding with square nails were also removed in order to add insulation and vinyl siding over the logs.

Over the years, the two original structures were joined together, and a new roof was simply put over the original shake roof of the kitchen. The shakes are still there above the original kitchen. Workers in the crawl space had an interesting time getting around. William and Jane added a screened-in porch as well as other rooms along the back side. Meacham Country Hams, established by William Meacham, is also located here.

As one drives up the long lane to our house or to visit Meacham Country Hams, one can imagine visitors driving up to the front door in a carriage on a circular drive that is no longer there. The family would have pulled in behind the two-story structure and unloaded goods and people in the open area between the kitchen and living area. This area is now the main entrance with a screened-in porch and a dining room.

The farm and home of Gary and Brenda Stenger at 1869 State Route 130, north of Morganfield, has been in Gary's family for six generations. The house (circa 1845) was originally a double log cabin consisting of four large rooms with a carriage drive between the two downstairs rooms and a loft area above connecting the two upstairs rooms. Each of the four main rooms included a working fireplace, served by a chimney on each end of the house. It was built by Raphael Cambron (1798–1883).

Raphael Cambron's son, Logan Christopher Cambron, a bachelor, was the main benefactor when St. Agnes Church was built in Uniontown. The land then passed to his daughter, Elizabeth Pauline Cambron Smith (1827–1913). Her daughter, Caroline Smith Proctor (1866–1932), and Elisha Edward Proctor (1864–1958) eventually deeded the farmstead to their son, Charles Smith ("Smith" or "C. S.") Proctor (1900–1961), who married Agnes Thomas (1899–1983) and moved there in 1920. Their daughter, Rita Proctor Stenger (1921–2000), rode her pony, Pearl, to St. Ann School every day, about five miles round trip.

In the 1930s, an addition to the back of the house was part of an extensive renovation and modernization. The update included two bathrooms, central heat (with a coal-fired boiler and radiators), and electricity in every room. The original sandstone back door step was moved to the end of the sidewalk beside the house and is still being used daily. One

of Rita's sons, Gary Proctor Stenger, his wife, Brenda Lovell Stenger, and their son, Thomas Jarrod, moved there in 1969. Their daughters, Tammie and Carrie, also grew up in this home. The family farm tradition is continuing into the eighth generation with Carrie's children, Coy and Cailey Divine.

The spring at the bottom of the hill was the main source of clean water on the farm for many years. In 1921, it was the first place electricity was installed in rural Union County and was used to pump water up the hill to the house. Just in front of the spring house is a concrete water trough and hand-pump formerly used to water the horses and mules. The wash house, one of two buildings directly behind the house, still has a working fireplace which was used to heat water for laundry and may have served as a summer kitchen. The large, old dinner bell was rung at mealtime and in case of emergencies. Its importance was eventually replaced by two-way radios and more recently by cell phones. Further up the hill is a small house originally built as a tenant house in the 1930s by the WPA/CCC. The "Lakehouse" is currently used for recreational purposes.

During the 1800s, there was enough corn and wheat production to feed the cattle and hogs on the original 189 acres. Corn that had been shocked was the main grain supply. There was some tobacco and lespedeza grown until the 1920s. To survive the Depression, Smith Proctor operated a Keck-Garnaman thrashing machine to custom-thrash wheat and seed for his neighbors. It was pulled and belt-driven by a gas-powered Keck-Garnaman tractor, the first rubber-tired tractor in the county. The original steel tires were exchanged with rubber ones (in the middle of Morton Street in Morganfield) in order to make it more mobile on county roads.

About this time, Smith Proctor also began a four-year crop rotation of his fields. To counteract the acid soils, he began spreading "lime" by hand with scoop shovels from wagons pulled by teams of mules. The first rotation was corn, followed by wheat interseeded with red clover, timothy, red top, and orchard grass. After the wheat was thrashed, cattle grazed in the stubble fields. During the third year, hay was cut and baled. After baling, the red clover was allowed to mature and was harvested for clover seed. During the fourth year, the field was used for pasturing cattle. By the 1950s, about 600 acres were on this four-year rotation plan and the corn was stored on the ear in corncribs and fed to the cattle and hogs. In 1962, the main corncrib burned after it was hit by lightning. The first two-row self-propelled Model A Gleaner combine (without a cab) was purchased and two 7,500-bushel Behlen grain bins were purchased from Edward O'Nan to store shelled corn. By the late 1970s, Gary and his brother, Thomas Proctor Stenger, formed a partnership and began planting

double-crop soybeans after wheat. After a tornado in 1979 destroyed most of the old grain bin system, the storage capacity was increased to 75,000 bushels and a 7,500-bushel-per-hour grain leg was installed. From 1980 to 1995, popcorn was also an important crop. In 1985, over one million pounds or approximately 75,000 bushels of popcorn were shipped by semi-truck to Wyandot Popcorn in Marion, Ohio. Today, corn and soybeans are the most important crops on the farm. The same fields which won a trophy back in 1930 for a high yield of thirty-six bushels of corn per acre are now averaging more than 175 bushels per acre and are being harvested by eight- and twelve-row combines.

Since the early 1800s, cattle have been an important part of the family history. There was always at least one milk cow on the farm, with the cows being milked by hand twice a day. The morning milk went to the owner's family and the evening milk was given to the farmhands. Gary's great-great-grandfather, George N. Proctor of rural Waverly, was credited with bringing the first purebred Shorthorn cattle to Union County. During the 1920s, both E. E. Proctor and Smith Proctor had large feedlots for cattle and hogs. The cattle were purchased and sold by rail car from Nashville to St. Louis and Kansas City in the west and Evansville and Chicago in the north. In 1926, there was a tour of the feedlot here as a part of a large Field Day associated with the eradication of "scrub" bulls in the county. Union County was the first county in the United States to receive this designation by the USDA. During the 1930s, the King Ranch sent three boxcar loads of Texas Longhorns and Brahman-influenced cattle here to try to isolate them from the hoof-and-mouth disease problems in Texas. Herefords were the main cattle breed for over one hundred years. About 1985, Gary decided to buy some Tarentaise cattle and created a new enterprise, Bluegrass Tarentaise. The cattle were shown at the Denver Stock Show for several years and purebred breeding stock have been sold as far away as the state of Washington.

Hogs also played an important role in the farm's history. Many of the hogs were sold, but others ended up being salt-cured in the old meat house, which unfortunately was lost to severe weather in 2011. Country ham stuffed with turnip greens was an Easter tradition for generations. Not only hams, but also shoulders, jowls, and bacon were salt-cured on the heavy wooden tables. Gary's grandmother, "Mom Proc," often sold salt-cured meat by the pound to neighbors and others who stopped by to get some "seasoning meat." (She also raised and sold frying chickens and eggs.) Lard was pressed into old crocks and lye soap was made for tough laundry stains. Fruitwood-smoked sausage is still a labor-intensive family tradition, as it has been every December for over 150 years.

RAMSEY CREEK FARM

Since the time of William Washington Brown, a South Carolina Presbyterian minister, seven generations of farmers and their families have lived on Ramsey Creek Farm. When the original house burned during the nineteenth century, a new house with three rooms was built on the same site and is still there today.

Through illnesses, sales, and inheritances, the farm has stayed in the family, increasing in size whenever possible. Dennie Gist Brown of the third generation bought property from several neighboring farms, including the Tate house, which is now occupied by Dennie, a great-grandson, and three great-great-grandchildren.

Oaklawn Farm, the home of Margaret Holt Chapman at 315 Voss Road near Sturgis, was the homeplace of her great-grandfather, Christopher C. Smith, and has been in the family since that time.

Christopher Smith was born in Delaware on November 28, 1812, and came to Union County in 1833. He purchased this farm in 1840 and lived on this site until his tragic death in 1880 at the hands of a disgruntled former slave.

Upon the death of Christopher Smith, the farm passed to his widow, Sarah Elizabeth Hall Smith, and his four children. Upon the death of Sarah Smith in 1913, one child was deceased and the 525 acres were inherited by son Will Smith and daughters Annie Marie and Bettie. In 1923, Will Smith died unmarried and the farm passed to his sisters Annie and Bettie, who had married brothers William and Thomas Holt. At that time the farm was divided between the two families, with the homeplace and 250 acres going to Annie and William H. Holt Sr. Upon the death of Annie in 1928, the land went to her sons, William H. Holt Jr. and Kenneth Holt, with William later buying out his brother Kenneth. After the death of William H. Holt Jr. in 1939 at age thirty-seven, the farm passed to his widow, Velma Small Holt, who was just twenty-six years old with three children. She held the farm for sixty years with tenants and farmhands, and later leased it. In the 1990s it was deeded to her children, Margaret Anne Holt Chapman, William Joseph Holt, and Kenneth David Holt. At this time some of the original farmland and the homeplace are still owned by Margaret Holt Chapman and the adjoining

farmland is owned by Dave Holt. Bill Holt sold his farm in 2009 to White Farms of Sturgis.

One original structure, a smokehouse and its contents, remains and is available for viewing on the tour. It was built circa 1840 of hand-hewn logs cut by slaves using pit saws and hand tools, with a foundation of sandstone hauled perhaps from Caseyville. Of special note are the square nails, which are still visible. Inside are the saltbox and a huge hollowed-out gum tree used to salt down the butchered meat. In the center of the room is the original fire pit for smoking the meat, and hanging above are four log slats (three original) for hanging the hams, shoulders, bacon, and sausage. A black iron pot for rendering fat into lard was used outside and then stored in the smokehouse after use. Three original pegs used to hang pigs for gutting and cutting are stored on one wall.

The original home of Christopher Smith at this site was a four-room log house of the same period. It was renovated in 1861 by a grand addition in the Federal style (shown in photographs and a watercolor). The house faced southward at that time, and the avenue and entry roads were what is now Holt Road. The rock step at the front gate, bearing the 1861 date of the renovation, is still visible. This was the home in which Margaret, Bill, and Dave were born. In the early morning hours of New Year's Day in 1938, the house burned to the ground, destroying generations of heirloom china, silver, pictures, furniture, and belongings. The children were aged five, three, and one. Later that year their father, William Holt, became ill and died the following June 1939.

Considerable improvements were done at Oaklawn Farm in 2000 when Margaret returned home and had a new house built by Steve Loxley on the site of the original Smith homeplace where she was born. Alan Vail did extensive restorations on the smoke-

house in 2000, shoring up the foundation and adding new chinking material between the logs. He also placed the hanging lanterns inside. The outside candle lanterns were purchased by Margaret at a historic replica shop at Monticello, Thomas Jefferson's home in Charlottesville, Virginia. New fences by M and M Fencing replaced the old wire-and-wood post fences that had deteriorated over time.

The home of Robert and Suzie Davis was built in 1820 and is believed to be the oldest brick home in Union County.

The home was built by William Harmon Davis. Mr. Davis' wife, Druzilla, opened a school for African American children after the Civil War.

The Davis family has occupied at least four farmhouses including the Old Brick House, the Homeplace, a house no one recalls except for a painting by B. S. Ross, and the wooden farmhouse now occupied by Hunter and Vicki Davis. The wooden farmhouse was built around 1870 and still has the original leaded glass and a claw-foot bathtub. Suzie Davis' great-grandfather, Withers, owned the house at one time.

The deed for the land where the house sits was signed by Patrick Henry. The iron swing in the side yard has been there for at least one hundred years.

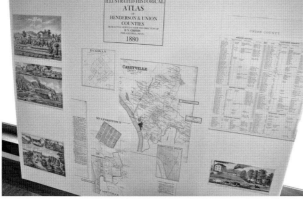

EIGHT GENERATIONS OF CULLENOOK FARM

Although it has only been known as Cullenook for the past thirty years, Cullenook Farm has a long history in Union County. The present-day operation comes from the former struggles of Cowan family ancestors dating back to the late 1700s. Jeremiah Cowan came from Ireland with his family, first to South Carolina, on to Tennessee, and later to Union County. He settled on land he had obtained between Boxville and Weaver City, now called Cullen. Jeremiah and his wife Elizabeth Hayes had several children and the Union County line descends from his son James W. Cowan. Jeremiah passed away in the 1820s and was interred in the Cowan-Holeman Cemetery, land he set aside for a family cemetery according to his will.

James W. Cowan received a portion of his father's land and continued a modest operation. James was also a preacher. He and others founded what is now the Pride Baptist Church in 1848. He married Catherine Carrier. James W. Cowan continued farming and preaching until his passing in 1883.

David Ervin Cowan was one of James and Catherine's children. He and his wife Rebecca Wynn lived out their lives modestly on the farm and also raised several children. We continue our lineage with their son Arnold.

Arnold Wayne Cowan also farmed land that he received as part of the family lineage. It is Arnold who is responsible for the present-day location of the Cullenook Farm. Just before the 1900s, Arnold met and married Nannie Mae Carrier. Her family farm joined a parcel Arnold owned. The young couple had a home on the main street in Cullen. Arnold was involved with road construction and seed and hardware

interests. Three of his sons, Arnold W. "Pike" Jr., Pete, and Clements, were successful on their own and with the Caterpillar Tractor Company. Clements Cowan brought one of the first Caterpillars to the area. Arnold was known for his teams of horses and mules and acquired up to thirteen teams in his heyday. Later he purchased an IHC Titan tractor. He farmed until his death in 1940.

Arnold's oldest surviving son, James W. "Jim" Cowan, was the patriarch of the present line. In 1921, Jim bought what is now the "homeplace." He also purchased a portion of the Carrier Farm that was once his mother's. Jim and his wife Nellie Christeen Lipford remodeled the small farmhouse that was once home to the town doctor. Working with his father and brothers, Jim built roads around the region. They never abandoned farming.

It was Jim and Nell who provided for what is now Cullenook Farm. Jim bought the farm's first viable farm tractor, a Ford 9N with accessories. This tractor and accessories are still in use on the farm today. Jim passed away in 1982, and Nell in 1988.

Jim and Nell's son Bobbie took over the land after Jim. He is responsible for the old barn's restoration and cleanup of some of the brushy areas of the farm. Bob, along with his wife Patsy Ann "Pat" Cates, helped provide support for farming endeavors. Bob also managed a trucking firm and Pat was associated with the schools and the Accuride Corporation. Bob and Pat continue to live on the site where Arnold's house once stood.

In 1980, Bob and Pat's son Michael and his wife Carole Marie Clements purchased the old house on the farm's corner. This structure was originally a store in the city of Cullen. It has since been remodeled and it now serves as their home and farm headquarters. Mike and Carole brought specialty crops to the farm. A greenhouse in the early nineties started what would become Cullenook Greenhouse. Carole, a farmer's daughter herself, loved growing flowers. Later this love of specialty crops led to produce. Cullenook Farm is also the home of Cowan Tractor Shop.

The year of 2010 saw the old farm change hands once more. Bob and Pat sold most of the land to Drennan Cowan, the youngest son of Michael and Carole. Drennan had been involved with the farm from his youth. He is now the eighth generation of Cowans to farm the Union County soil. He has been committed to the greenhouse and specialty crops found at the farm. While still a student at Western Kentucky University in Bowling Green, Drennan purchased the farm from his grandparents. He also purchased the land across the road, adding a grain system, machinery storage, and doubling the farm acreage. He plans to add vineyards and orchards to the farm.

Cullenook Farm now grows vegetables using the latest techniques and GAP practices available. To provide a safe and inexpensive venue for children, agritourism was added to the farm's operations. In the fall, the old hills come alive with the laughter of children and adults alike as they peruse the pumpkin patch looking for that perfect pumpkin. A corn maze, hayride, and other attractions have also been added. Cullenook also founded the county's first CSA (Community Supported Agriculture) program. Jim and Nell's home, where their daughter Audrey now resides, is also home to Cullenook Creations, a custom design and embroidery operation. Audrey's sons, Dalton, Landon, Mason, and Logan, also help with the produce and agritourism. They represent the ninth generation.

LAND O'NAN FARMS

Still Operating After 143 Years

Elisha Harmon died in 1868 and willed tracts of land to his niece, Martha Harmon, on the condition that she would not marry her neighbor and suitor. So, Martha Harmon married John Thomas O'Nan and inherited the western Kentucky land in 1871. She had three sons, John Lee, Dennis Edward, and George Oscar O'Nan. Dennis Edward O'Nan had a son named Charles Rhea O'Nan. In 1948, Charles Rhea bought out his uncle John Lee. Later he purchased the land that belonged to his other brother's heir, Mary Edna O'Nan. Charles Rhea and his wife Dottie have two children, Marsha and Adam.

Adam and his wife Kristi live and farm on the homeplace. The home was built in 1868. The logs from the original homeplace now make up the family room.

WELLS BROTHERS FARMS

Four Generations of Farming

Walter Wells bought 58.5 acres in Pride from E. L. and Eula Lynn in 1919. He came to Union County from Logan County at the age of two with his mother and father, a twin brother, and six other brothers and sisters. Farming was his life as he grew up. He walked and dropped corn and drove a horse that pulled a rock to cover the corn. He also worked in the tobacco fields. He was not able to attend school until he was ten and then only when there wasn't any work to be done. He could also be found delivering mail for the Pony Express from Bordley to Dixon, around eighteen miles, for one dollar per day until his contract ended in 1900. At the age of twenty-two and with $3.50 in his pocket, he married Effie Carter. He sold his horse, rented a house in Morganfield, and worked at the ice plant for $1.25 per day. He saved his money and bought a team of mules and rented a farm. In 1919, he bought his first farm of 58.5 acres and during the next several years worked at farming, coal mining, and other jobs while buying more land and paying for it. He bought his first tractor in 1931. He helped build the railroad through Pride in 1904, using mules with no machinery. He always had great love and respect for the land. He passed this love of the land to three of his five sons, Charles, Spencer, and Sam. At the age of ninety-three, he was still driving a tractor.

Spencer's son Joe Walt Wells lives on the original homeplace with his wife Patty. They have remodeled Walter's home many times and added a striking pool, patio, and outdoor fireplace where one can enjoy the backdrop of lush fields of corn and beans. They have two children, Drew and Mitzi.

Four generations later, Walter Mark Wells is farming in the Pride community. He farms with Ray, Clay, Camron, and Roger Wells. The farming operation has expanded since 1919 and is now called Wells Brothers Farms after Ray and Roger. Mark bought his first farm and home in 2009 after graduating from Western Kentucky University.

Today's technology has changed everything. The combine and four-wheel drive tractors are equipped with John Deere Green Star technology. This software tracks and records coordinates, farms, seed, planting, and harvest data that are uploaded onto home computers for further analysis and recordkeeping. The fifth generation of the family is just starting. It seems the love of the Pride farmland remains intact. Time will tell.

McCOUGHTRY FARM

McCoughtry Farm is located in Union County, Kentucky, and is owned by Sue Ellen Hoheimer. The farm was originally purchased in 1795 by Sarah McCoughtry. It was a Revolutionary War land grant to Uriah Springer patented to John Lewis and then assigned to Sarah McCoughtry. William and Sarah McCoughtry, Sue's great-great-great-grandparents, obtained the farm in 1819 and 1826.

As the McCoughtry family was preparing to leave Virginia before 1820, early deeds were being recorded in Union County laying claim to their new land. A Revolutionary War land grant of 1,000 acres was the reason for the McCoughtry family's journey into this wilderness. They traveled down the Monongahela and Ohio rivers on a flatboat carrying William, Sarah, and three children. William's long rifle, which had survived an early war, would now provide food for his growing family. The course charted by the navigator of the flatboat would bring them within a mile and a half of their new home site near the Ohio River in Union County, Kentucky.

A small cabin was built to house the family until the late 1820s, when a permanent cabin, one some sixty by twenty feet and two stories high, would be erected of cypress logs. Before 1838, a new kitchen and dining room were built and connected to the cabin by a hallway. This wing was built with wood from the land and brick made from the nearby Clay Pond. The ash wood from the old flatboat was recycled and is still in use today as the dining room floor. A large cherry wood poster bed made by William McCoughtry before 1838 is in the front bedroom of the old log cabin—a masterpiece by any cabinetmaker's standards. It remains in use today.

The McCoughtrys' mill across the road from the Big House was visited by Abraham Lincoln to grind corn. Early letters to Miss Eliza McCoughtry from Mr. Lincoln have regrettably been lost over the years. The Old Mill is now history but the millstone has been preserved.

The land William and Sarah owned would be divided among their seven living children around 1860. The land was passed down from one generation to the next with one stipulation: that the name "McCoughtry Farm" would be used.

The McCoughtry School and Chapel was used by the children of the community as a school during the week and as a place of worship on Sunday. The school continued from the 1890s until the 1940s. Penelope Ann Hoheimer, who attended the school as a small child, was the fifth generation to live on the land, she being the great-great-granddaughter of William and Sarah McCoughtry.

Cherry wood was cut from the farm to be used for caskets for family members buried in the nearby Reburn Cemetery. The family plot also has a marker for a family servant named "Aunt Kesire." A dining room sideboard was said to be constructed of cherry wood that was left over from the construction of one of the old caskets. Old cherry wood, aged for about one hundred years, was also used to panel the hallway in the 1940s.

Sometime before the year 1897, the log house was covered with weather board and a porch was built across the front with gingerbread trim. This was done by Sarah "Sally" McCoughtry. Also at this time, oak woodwork was put over the entire front of the house with a pretty oak stairway, all of which are still in use.

In 1942, Katherine Lewis Taylor remodeled the house, taking down two upstairs bedrooms on opposite sides of the house. Green shutters were added and the house was painted white. In 1950, Katherine remodeled the kitchen and dining room and also covered the old brick walls with new brick veneer. Additions were made in the 1960s, including one room built from the log cabin of Fielding Jones, the first white man to permanently settle in Union County. In 1978, the front of the house was bricked over, making the entire house brick.

Over 400 acres of the original acreage, including the log homestead, have been occupied by the same family for over 170 years. McCoughtry Farm today produces corn, soybeans, and wheat. Hereford cattle have been on the farm since 1897. At that time, Tom Lewis, husband of Penelope McCoughtry and father of Katherine Lewis Taylor, purchased the first breeding stock from White County, Illinois.

Each generation living in the house made changes appropriate to their time, but inside the walls of the old house, at its core, the cypress logs placed by the first McCoughtrys still remain.

A special thank-you to Mrs. A. G. Pritchett and Mr. Peyton Heady for their time and effort spent in helping to compile this material and history of McCoughtry Farm.

ROBERTANNA FARM

Robertanna Farm originally consisted of 120 acres, located on what is now Highway 141 North, a few miles west of Waverly, Kentucky. The acreage, which was then covered with timber and partial wetlands, was purchased by Robert Lee and Anna Clements Roberts in 1895.

They were the parents of ten children, Lewis Sidney, Robert William, Lillian Roberts Pfeffer, George, Sue Roberts Buckman Presser, Lucy Roberts Clements, Sister Robert Mary of Nazareth, John Francis, Florence A. Roberts, and Agnes Roberts Clements.

After the untimely death of Robert Lee Roberts in 1918, operation of the farm was taken over by his second-oldest son, Robert William, known as "R. W." Lewis. The oldest son had already left home to pursue an education in medicine, and later made his home in Kansas. R. W. married Frances Margaret Roberts in June 1922. She was the daughter of John Christopher and Matilda Clements Roberts. The farm continued to grow through various purchases made by R. W. and Frances. The largest parcel, being 260 acres, was purchased in 1945 and was then known as the Spaulding Place. This land was also home to one of the county's oldest and most historic houses, the brick Spaulding home, which was built in 1850.

R. W. received the Master Conservationist Award in 1945 for being a firm believer of conservation, using tiles, diversion ditches, and catch basins long before it was a common Union County farming practice.

Ruth Helen, daughter of R. W. and Frances, was born on May 3, 1923. She attended St. Vincent Academy for twelve years. At that time, the main form of transportation was on horseback, and Ruth Helen rode her pony three miles up a dirt road every day to and from school. The family was of strong Catholic faith and attended

Sacred Heart Catholic Church, which was located a few miles away by the Academy. It is the same church that Ruth Helen and her family still attend today.

In 1945, Ruth Helen married Edward C. Espy of Indianapolis, Indiana. They operated the farm in partnership with R. W. and Frances Roberts. During the 1950s, they expanded the livestock operation. Ed served on the formation committee of the Union County Water District. The nearby historic Spaulding home was refurbished and became the Espys' family home.

Ed and Ruth Helen's son, Edward Charles Espy II, was born in January 1948. Eddie, as he is known, graduated from St. Vincent Academy in 1966 and attended the University of Kentucky. In 1968, he married Judy Woodruff, the daughter of Harry and Amelia Graves Woodruff of Morganfield. In 1970, Eddie, the fourth generation of Robertanna Farm, began practicing new livestock and crop genetics, implementing new techniques such as no-tilling and minimum tillage.

Laura Ann, the daughter of Eddie and Judy, was born in 1974 and is the fifth generation to continue the Robertanna Farm heritage. Laura graduated from Union County High School in 1992 and Western Kentucky University in 1996. On May 18, 1996, Laura married Eddie Wheatley, the son of Malcolm and Leslie Wheatley of Waverly. The legacy of Robertanna Farm is being passed on through Laura and Eddie as they begin the sixth generation with their children, Audrey Morgan, Caroline Grace, Anna Claire, Olivia Rose, Waylon Grant Edward, and Claudia Ann Wheatley.

Through the past 116 years, Robertanna Farm has expanded to a productive 670-acre corn and soybean crop operation, reaching yields and implementing modern technology those earlier generations could have only dreamed of.

BILLY DON AND JOYCE CARROLL GREENWELL FARM

The Billy Don and Joyce Carroll Greenwell Farm is located two miles north of Waverly, Kentucky, on Highway 669. Billy Don's great-great-grandparents, Robert and Rebecca Walker Hancock, bought this farm in 1854. The original 254 acres are still included in this farm. A log cabin was built first and then a much larger farmhouse was built around the log cabin in the late 1800s. This farmhouse was torn down in 1978 and is now the location of the farm shop, grain bins, barns, and former hog operation.

Some antique light fixtures were saved from the old home and are now restored and in use by Billy Don and Joyce's children in their homes.

Billy Don and Joyce purchased the farm in 1970 with Billy Don's brothers, Tommy and Gerald. In 1972, Billy Don bought the farm from his brothers.

The farm produces corn, soybeans, and hay and has a cattle operation. Billy Don is still active in the farm operation along with his sons, Ralph, Jason, Paul, and Bryan.

NORRIS FAMILY FARM

Samuel Norris arrived in Union County around 1824 with a group of Catholics led by Elisha Durbin (a priest) from Nelson County, Kentucky. Samuel was married to Margaret Payne and had five daughters and one son. He died at an early age in 1837. He left a will stating that when his son, James Rowan, came of age, enough of Samuel's belongings were to be sold to make one hundred dollars for his inheritance.

Norris Family Farm

At the age of thirty, James Rowan Norris bought 224 acres in Henshaw close to St. Ambrose Church. It was bought at the courthouse door for $1,508.80. He married Frances Hedges and had six children, Virginia, Emma, Mary, James, Samuel, and Frances. In 1910, the farm was transferred to Samuel Omer Norris. Samuel Omer was married to Ethel Alvey and they had two children, Samuel Robert "Bob" and Mary Frances Norris. In 1973, the farm was transferred to Bob Norris. Bob Norris is married to Erma Vickery Norris and they have three children, Samuel Ray, Karla Norris Higdon, and Robert Russell.

Samuel Ray married Norma Bumpus and they have three daughters, Melanie, Cindy, and Deidra. They moved to the Norris family farm in the 1970s and will be its next owners.

MADGE LUCKETT FARM

Louis P. Clements, father of the current owner, Madge C. Luckett, purchased a 275-acre tract of land from Will Tom Wathen in 1901. The existing large two-story house was built at that time. Louis Clements lived on the farm through the births of his eight children, Christine (Sister Carmel), George Louis, Alice, Sam, Flora "Chrissy," Pat, Madge, and Paul. Madge was born in the farmhouse in 1915.

Louis P. Clements sold the land to Leo Luckett and Madge in 1942. Leo and Madge were forced to move from their Union County property, which later became part of Camp Breckinridge. Until his death in 1973, Leo farmed the land with an eye toward conservation, using the most up-to-date fertilization and agricultural practices. His farming expertise was widely known as evidenced by the many awards he received, such as Master Conservationist, Master Pastureman, and numerous write-ups in farm magazines.

Since 1973, Madge, ninety-six, continues to manage the farm with the capable help of her son, Ronald Luckett, and her farm manager, Ronald Davis. Inspired by Leo and Madge's farming practices, Mr. Davis continues to maintain a nice balance between livestock and crops, including the growing of corn, soybeans, wheat, and alfalfa hay and the raising of cattle, all of which have contributed to a stable agricultural environment in the past and will for the future.

From 1948 to 1969, the raising of registered hogs (Hampshire and Landrace) was a big part of the farming operation. In addition, Leo and Madge maintained a sizable chicken operation, raising up to 500 laying hens. The eggs were sold directly from the farm to drive-up customers and to local egg handling/distribution establishments. Leo and Madge were also widely recognized for the raising and breeding of registered Polled Shorthorn cattle. The genetics of the current crossbred cows here, which number about fifty head, can be traced back to a large extent to Polled Shorthorn cows and an outstanding Polled Shorthorn bull, which was named the 1947 International Grand Champion.

In addition to the house, two original outbuildings remain on the property: the carbide house (lighting provided by carbide), later called the egg house, and the buggy house, later called the garage. Both buildings are currently being maintained and used as storage facilities.

HIRAM McELROY SR. FARM

The original McElroy Farm owner was Hiram McElroy Sr., who left the farm to his sons, Hiram Jr. and Hugh. The original Hiram McElroy home has been gone for more than a century, but the sons' homes still stand. The Hiram McElroy Jr. home is located at the end of the McElroy subdivision and is now owned and occupied by Donna Graham. The Hugh McElroy home is owned by the McElroy farming corporation (McElroy Heirs, LLC) and is occupied by Helen McElroy.

Hiram and Hugh had several children. All of the McElroys presently from Union County are from Hiram's side of the family. Hiram's three youngest sons were Caswell, Roscoe, and Clarence. They inherited most of the farmland. Only Roscoe's land remains in the family. One of the older brothers was also named Hiram. He was a surveyor on the Panama Canal project. Once the project was completed, he never returned to Kentucky, but settled in Tampa, Florida.

Roscoe left his part of the family farm to his only child, John B. McElroy (husband of Helen). John's children, John C. "J.C." Hugh, and Karen, inherited the farm from their father.

John C. McElroy currently manages the farm and operates a cow/calf operation on part of the farm. The cropland is currently rented to his cousin Jim McElroy and John's son Doug.

The family is not sure what year Hiram came to Union County, but he was the first state representative from this county to represent Union County in Frankfort. This is documented in the book *The History of Union County*.

Pow Wow

Representatives from the Cherokee, Shawnee, and Navajo tribes gathered at the Uniontown City Park for a traditional pow wow. A pow wow is an intertribal gathering of Native Americans who gather to socialize, dance, sing, and honor their cultures. Others who are not Native American are often invited to attend in order to learn about tribal history and traditions and for entertainment. Since drugs, fighting, alcohol, and swearing are not allowed, this makes the pow wows good-natured and peaceful gatherings of friends.

Participants wore colorful costumes. Vendors provided food and crafts for purchase.

This Bicentennial Celebration event was sponsored by the City of Uniontown, Eidetik, Earle C. Clements Job Corps Academy, Kenny Kent Chevrolet, Floyd's Supermarket, Jim David Meats, Clements Discount Drugs, O'Nan Body Shop, Red Hat Realty, French's Supermarket, Walmart, Sturgis True Value, Ace House of Carpets, Sturgis Food Giant, Dr. William C. Tapp, Vaughn, Geiger and Associates, Uniontown Food Mart, KTS Smoke, Dr. David Starkey, Dr. Tim Joiner, Sturgis Family Dollar, Tri-County Waste, Unique Boutique Salon, ALPS, Shouse Farms, Morganfield Lions Club, Kentucky Utilities Company, and Union County First.

DAVY CROCKETT AND THE RIVER PIRATES COME TO TOWN

Moviegoers were treated to a rare presentation of *Davy Crockett and the River Pirates* at the Sturgis Amphitheatre on Friday evening and the Renaissance Corner in Morganfield on Saturday evening. This movie, which was originally supposed to be a television episode, was made in 1955 on the Ohio River near Cave in Rock, Illinois. Several local residents had bit parts in the movie.

During the filming of the movie, the actors stayed in the three motels (Bel-Air Motel, Forty Winks Motel, and The New Capitol Hotel) in Morganfield. Fess Parker, who played

Davy Crockett, stayed in Room 11 in the Bel-Air Motel. It is said that young fans camped outside the motel to have the opportunity to get Mr. Parker's autograph and followed the film crew around the area as they made preparations for filming the movie.

Vendors provided food for this movie showing. Both showings drew a large crowd.

This Bicentennial Celebration event was sponsored by the Sturgis Antique Mall, the City of Morganfield, and the Union County Bicentennial Committee.

Bash BACK TO SCHOOL

August 13, 2011

Families enjoyed the afternoon playing on inflatables in the Bicentennial Park. Refreshments were also available.

This Bicentennial Celebration event was sponsored by Downtown Morganfield, Inc.

PRIDE·OF THE
Counties

Many volunteers made it possible for Union County to have a booth at the Kentucky State Fair. The theme for the booth was highlighting the Bicentennial Celebration and pictures from the events that had already been held were on display. Door prizes were donated by several businesses and organizations from Union County.

The Pride of the Counties is sponsored by the Kentucky Farm Bureau and the Kentucky State Fair to promote Kentucky counties. Displays from participating counties were in one area, making it convenient for fairgoers to see just what Kentucky has to offer.

CORN FESTIVAL TRAP SHOOT

September 11, 2011

Over forty shooters of all ages gathered at the Twin Silos Shooting Complex near Sturgis to participate in this Bicentennial Celebration event. Wearing eye and ear protection and carrying shells and shotguns, these individuals competed in various age and gender categories for trophies.

The opening ceremony included the welcome, the stating of the safety rules to be followed, and a thank-you to the sponsors and donors. The Pledge of Allegiance and the 4-H Pledge were recited, and the National Anthem was sung. A moment of silence was observed in memory of those who lost their lives in the terrorist attack on this day ten years ago.

In the Trap Shoot, the first-place winners in individual categories were:

Youth Division: Tyler Buckman
Women's Division: Lynda Jackson
Men's Division: Chat Young

The first-place team winners were:
Youth Division: Tyler Buckman, Rhett Caldwell, Drake Gibbs, Cayne Young, and Dakota Jones
Women's Division: Lynda Jackson, Cindy Jones, Monica Wright, and Annette Buckman
Men's Division: Doug Omer, Rick Jackson, Chat Young, Rob Hagan, and Dalton Rutter

Refreshments were available for purchase.

This Bicentennial Celebration event was sponsored by Union County Shooting Sports, Inc.

BICENTENNIAL PARK DEDICATION

September 15, 2011

A large crowd gathered for the dedication of the Bicentennial Park across from the Union County Courthouse. Beautifully landscaped on all four sides, the park is a beautiful addition to downtown Morganfield.

The east side of the park displays the beautiful Quilt Blocks that are on the rear wall of the Union County Public Library.

The Memorial Tree Garden on the south side hill of the park displays oak, American blooming cherry, and lilac trees that were planted in memory or honor of: Christopher Columbus Smith, Iva and Wayne Waggener, Jane Truitt Bell and Jane Roy Bell, Jim Voss, Malcolm Hart, the Steward and Humphrey families, Dane Thomsen Holeman, Larry Joe and Jody Jenkins, Tommy Luckett, and the Bicentennial Committee members.

The west side of the park is landscaped with various flowering bushes between the parking lot and the new brick street.

The north side of the park facing the courthouse has five sections. Four sections are landscaped with various flowering bushes, including roses. The middle section displays the "Tree of Life" statue and is landscaped. Two decorative benches sit in front of the four sections.

In the middle of the parking lot, which has parking spaces for twenty-two vehicles, are two islands that have decorative bushes and ornamental lamplights.

The artist's rendition of the "Tree of Life" statue was unveiled. The seven-by-six-foot statue would depict the qualities that have made our community what it is today: family, faith, diversity, community, education, river, coal, agriculture, and industry. A replica of the Bicentennial Emblem is also on the "Tree of Life." When the statue was placed in the middle section, a time capsule containing items from the Bicentennial Celebration events was included.

REDEDICATION OF THE BULL ROCK MONUMENT

September 15, 2011

Union County attracted nationwide attention in 1926 when it became the first county in the United States to have only purebred bulls, as a result of a campaign that had

started four years earlier. The product of this influx of purebred stock and the subsequent publicity made it a notable event in the livestock chapter of Union County's history.

A scrub sire eradication program began with a committee of seven men who drew up the procedures of the program. They were W. W. Sugg, Clarence McElroy, Charles Meacham Jr., Len Daniel, B. L. Conway, K. G. Davis, and W. M. Quirey, with assistance from Wayland Rhoads, extension agent in beef cattle production, and R. O. Wilson, county agent.

A bronze plaque recognizing this accomplishment was presented to Union County by the Louisville Board of Trade. It was mounted on a rock which came from "The Rocks" area between the "Y" Community and Shawneetown, Illinois.

At one time, the monument was relocated near the Odd Fellows Cemetery because some of the war memorial ladies felt the monument was offensive. The decision was later made to move the monument back to the courthouse lawn, where it is today.

Dr. Darrah Bullock, a professor of animal science and breeding at the University of Kentucky, talked of how the scrub sire eradication program has made for a much better understanding of heritability, and how using better parents makes for better offspring. This will enable the following generations of cattle farmers to have greater production and consumer quality. Additional remarks were made by Gary Stenger, local cattleman and farmer, and Rankin Powell, Union County extension agent.

CORN FESTIVAL

September 15–17, 2011

Once again the Corn Festival drew a large crowd to Morganfield to celebrate Corn Festival weekend. Food and craft booths, game booths, carnival rides, contests, the soapbox derby, balloon artistry, special music, Bingo, special entertainment by Skip Bond and the Fugitives, and, of course, the grand finale, the Corn Festival Parade, provided for great entertainment throughout the weekend.

Tamara Stevens was crowned 2011 Miss Corn Festival. The first runner-up was Megan Greenwell. Rena Mayes was chosen as Miss Congeniality by the other contestants.

The Miss Teen Corn Festival winner was Morgan Duncan with Kaylin Davis being Miss Congeniality.

Miss Pre-Teen Corn Festival was won by Aubree Mills with second place going to Lauren Willett and third place going to Sierra Tipton. Prettiest Smile went to Emily Hibbs and Miss Congeniality to Jacqueline Davis.

The Little Miss Corn Festival winner was Kyla Burke with Anna Ervin coming in second and Jayla Ricketts coming in third.

The Little Mr. Corn Festival winner was Colin Nalley with Kyle Capps coming in second and Caden Polites coming in third.

The youngest girls and boys had their chance to be winners too. In the Under 6 Months category, the winners were Zayleah Burnette and Rylan Pierson. In the 7 to 12 Months category, the winners were Ava Mills and Connor Cowan. In the 13 to 18 Months category, the winners were Nia Morris and Conner Chandler. Kalayah Henshaw and Conner Yates were the winners in the 19 to 24 Months category. Gavin Grimes and Gabriel Escalera placed first in the 2 to 3 Years Old category. Lilly Hibbs and Dusten Trent were the winners in the 4 to 5 Years Old category.

In the talent contest, Isaac Coomes placed first with his a capella singing and dancing to Justin Bieber's song "Baby."

The soapbox derby was a favorite of boys and girls who raced their cars downhill in an attempt to post winning times in the event.

Grand Marshall for this year's parade was Captain Bill Crow, U.S. Navy (Ret.), a native of Morganfield. Captain Crow graduated from the United States Naval Academy in 1980. During his thirty years of service at sea and ashore, he received five Navy and Marine Corps Commendation Medals, two Navy and Marine Corps Achievement Medals, and five Meritorious Service Medals.

Golden Kernel Honorees were Tommy and Allegra Luckett for their devoted service to Union County. Tommy served as a county judge from 1963 to 1978, and with his wife owned the Dairy Maid in Morganfield from 1957 to 1977. They provided many summer jobs for the teenagers of Union County, and the Dairy Maid was a popular place to hang out for kids of all ages. They are actively involved in the Senior Citizens Program in Morganfield.

Numerous floats crafted by businesses, churches, organizations, and school clubs provided for a lengthy parade that started at the Legion Park and made its way through downtown Morganfield. Farm machinery, horses, classic vehicles, and the Union County High School band made great additions to the parade. The Morganfield Police Department even had a chance to show off its new SUV.

The winner of the top parade prize was the Morganfield Home Center with its float featuring a rotating twenty-five-cent coin with the Bicentennial Emblem on one side and the bust of George Washington on the other. Other winners were:

    Business Category: River View Coal Mine

    School Category: Union County 4-H Corn Dog Races

    Church Category: Grove Center Faith Chapel

    Civic Category: Patriotic Timeline Parade Association

HISTORICAL SITE RECOGNIZED

September 17, 2011

What is so special about 101 East Main Street in Morganfield? It was the first plot to be laid out on the plat map of Morganfield in 1811. The original building on this lot housed the Capitol Hotel and People's Bank and Trust. The hotel's top two floors were eventually torn down and the bank portion of the building was remodeled. When the bank moved to a more modern building some years ago, Martin McElroy and Tom Duncan purchased the building for use as their offices.

The Union County Bicentennial Committee presented a plaque to Mr. McElroy and Mr. Duncan designating 101 East Main Street as an official Morganfield Bicentennial Site.

The John Arnold Arena at the fairgrounds was the scene for this three-day celebration, which featured a horse show, speed horse events, trail trials, and open team roping. A large crowd of spectators, exhibitors, and participants made this event a huge success. Evelyn Meacham stated, "There have been so many people who come up to me and say what a great event this is, and we're really proud of the celebration and the support we have received from the county."

Speed trials consisted of pole racing, barrel races, and flag and plug racing. This event was sanctioned by the National Barrel Horse Association, so it drew more than 300 entries. Winners shared approximately $5,600 in prize money.

The horse show had entries from Western to English, pleasure to reining, and gaited to hunters. The trail trial

set the course for pacing horses to open and close gates, walk across bridges, jump over a fallen log, cross water, and cross a seesaw. All of these items represent challenges that horses may come across while on a backwoods trail. Participants competed for cash prizes.

A wonderful treat was watching the Union County 4-H Equine Drill Team and the State Champion and Reserve Champion 4-H drill teams perform. History displays on horses in Union County were available. Also on display were close to one hundred saddles that represented championship saddles, handmade seat saddles, and historic sidesaddles. Visitors enjoyed demonstrations, horseshoeing, and wagon and pony rides.

A BBQ supper was available for purchase on Saturday evening. Bill Johnson, a local musician, provided entertainment.

This Bicentennial Celebration event was sponsored by several Union County merchants and the Union County Fiscal Court.

The Homemakers Clubs from Sturgis and Henshaw celebrated the Bicentennial by visiting the residents at the Sturgis Nursing Home. After a brief history of the county was presented, everyone enjoyed refreshments and gifts.

People of all ages visited the John Arnold Arena at the Sturgis Fairgrounds to see displays presented by personnel from several coal companies and coal-related agencies. They were able to hear lectures on the importance of coal, jobs in the coal industry, and how they could become part of that industry. There were displays of mining equipment that have been used through the years and demonstrations and competitions by the miners. Everyone attending was able to see just how far the coal industry has progressed through the years.

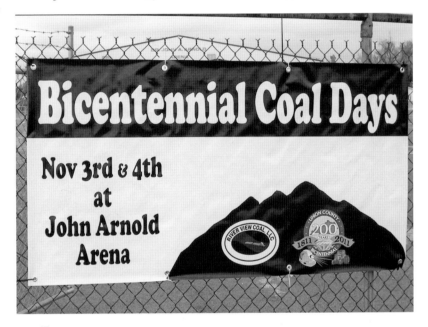

Eighteen seams of coal of varying thicknesses lie beneath the surface of Union County. Five of them are considered major veins: the Baker (No. 13), Paradise (No. 12), Herrin (No. 11), Springfield (No. 9), and Davis (No. 6) seams. The earliest known commercial mine in Union County was formed in 1853 and became known as the Kentucky Coal Company. The mine and resulting mining town, called Curlew, was situated between Caseyville and DeKoven. The original founder and part owner of the mine was President John Tyler, who visited the site.

During our county's bicentennial period, a stretch of 200 years, numerous mines have come and gone. In the 1980s, three Peabody Camp Complex mines situated near Waverly, along with three Island Creek mines situated around Uniontown, employed 3,000 miners. Millions of tons of coal were mined during this period. Three state-of-the-art mines are currently operating in Union County: Dodge Hill Mining, LLC Mine No. 1, located near Sturgis; Highland Mining Company, LCC, located near Waverly; and River View Coal, LCC, located near Uniontown. Union County is the number-two producer of coal in the Western Kentucky Coal Field.

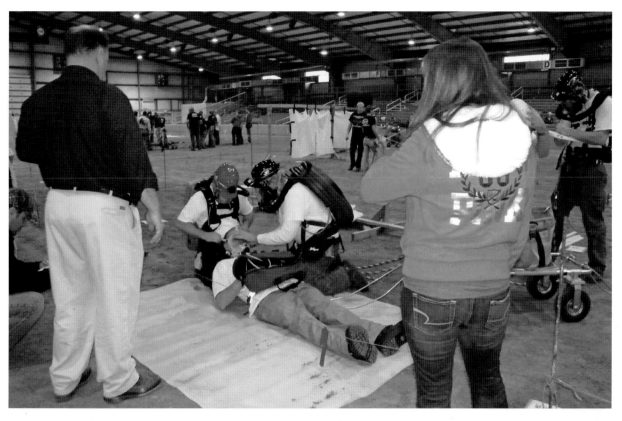

The public had a rare opportunity to visit some of Morganfield's oldest homes when Downtown Morganfield, Inc., hosted the Historic Home Tour.

Quentin and Hildegarde Wesley's home at 220 South Morgan Street was built in 1892 by Jim Taylor. Mrs. Goldie Leiter was the original owner of the home and lived there until her death. J. K. Waller purchased the home and lived there with his family until 1969. The Wesleys purchased the home from Mr. Waller.

Keith and Julie Gough's home at 300 South Morgan Street was built in 1885 by H. D. Allen. Upon his death, the home passed to his heirs, H. D. Allen Jr., G. Blanton Allen, Bessie J. Allen, and Martha Allen. A. B. "Red" and Thelma Davis purchased the home in 1955. After their deaths, the home was left to Glenna Waller Calvin in 1997. In 2000, Frank and Julie Morgan purchased the home and lived there until 2006, when they sold it to Scott and Sarah Galante. The Goughs purchased the home in 2009.

Phyllis Garrett's home at 510 East Main Street is on property originally purchased by Hamner Morton around 1907. In 1910, Mr. Morton hired Harris and Shopbell, architects from Evansville, to design a home for the property. Mr. Morton lived in the house until he died. The house then went to his son, Elliott Morton, who lived there until his death. He left the house to his daughter, Jane. Clarence and Phyllis Garrett purchased the home in 1977 and raised their three children there.

220 South Morgan Street

300 South Morgan Street

510 East Main Street

520 West Main Street

312 West Main Street

The home at 520 West Main Street was built around 1900 for Dr. Richards. The lumber was cut from the Richards' woods and features lovely stained glass and oak and black walnut woodwork. Over the years, this home has been used as a funeral parlor and by South Central Bell. Arthur Veatch bought the home from Dr. Richards. In 1966, Jerry and Jeanette Manning purchased the home and sold it to Frank and Carolyn Eiter in 1976. The current owners of the home are David and Maribeth Logsdon, who purchased the home in 1991 from the Eiters.

Built in 1904, Dennis and Susan Kirchner's home at 312 West Main Street was originally owned by Susan's great-great-grandmother, Maggie Berry. She passed the home down to her daughter, Lillian Wright, who in turn passed the home down to Tom Harris, who was Susan's father. This home has been in the family for 150 years. The home was designed by Harris and Shopbell of Evansville and cost $2,730.

The home at 228 West Main Street was completed around 1901 for Aaron Waller Mason. After his death, his son, Gordon, and his wife occupied the home. The home remained in the Mason family until it was purchased in 1964 by Earl and Viola Bohnencamp. In 2008, Eidetik purchased the home, and after completely renovating it, continues to use it for their office. Architects Harris and Shopbell of Evansville also designed this home.

James Mason Dyer built the home at 410 East Main Street in 1895. The home has remained in the Dyer family for several generations. Orville and Sally Dyer purchased the home and lived there until their deaths. Their son, Jim, acquired the home in 1994, and currently lives there with his wife, Rebecca. They have completed extensive renovations and have worked to preserve the charm and grace of this old family home.

The home of David and Melissa Beaven at 304 West Main Street was completed around 1903 and was built for Charles Jones Newman and his wife, Camilla Mason Newman. When Camilla died in 1939, A. V. and Catherine Conway purchased the home and the home remained in the Conway family until the early 1990s. This is yet another home designed by Harris and Shopbell of Evansville.

228 West Main Street

410 East Main Street

304 West Main Street

A GRAND BALL HONORING UNION COUNTY'S BICENTENNIAL

The Camp Breckinridge Museum and Arts Center was the backdrop for the Grand Bicentennial Ball. A large crowd danced to the music of The Lost Boys and enjoyed a night of socializing with friends.

The "Tree of Life" at the Bicentennial Park was officially dedicated in front of a large crowd. Rev. Jerry Manning gave the invocation. Remarks were made by County Judge Executive Jody Jenkins; Union County Public Library District Director Debbie McClanahan; Kim Humphrey, chairperson of the Bicentennial Committee; and Joe Bell, member of the Bicentennial Committee.

The roots of the Tree pay tribute to the foundation of Union County: family, coal, agriculture, river, education, industry, diversity, community, and faith. In the center of the Tree is a replica of the Bicentennial Emblem. Prior to the placement of the "Tree of Life," a time capsule was placed in the ground. In the time capsule were items that depicted the different events of the Bicentennial Celebration.

The last event of the Union County Bicentennial Celebration was the dedication of the Quilt Blocks displayed on the back wall of the Union County Public Library. Melanie Bealmear with the University of Kentucky Cooperative Extension Service read the names of those to whom the Quilt Blocks were placed in their memory or in their honor:

Blackie McLeod	Nash and Ann Monsour
Robert and Dru Adamson	Joe and Mary Ellen Buckman
Ruth and Newt Morgan	Agnes Rowley Woodruff
Collins and May Hosman	Shirley Mercer
Faye Davis Joyner	Fannie Brown
Allie Wallace and Hilda Potts	Margaret Girvin
The Wise Families of Union County	Ruth Thomas
Persis Hart	Lucille Pickens Babbs
O. P. and Sallianna Dyer	Roger and Martha Adamson
Dot Timmons	James D. Veatch
Edward O'Nan	Leva Parish
Florine Johnson	Thomas E. Simpson
Charles Morgan	Madeline Shelton
The Marvel Family	Mae Moore
Norma Jean Martin	

The Quilt Blocks are a beautiful addition to the Bicentennial Park. More blocks will be added as they are received.

We ended our Bicentennial year with a ball; a Bicentennial Ball, that is.

The year 2011 was a great and fantastic year with many celebrations and tremendous activities. The entire county entered into the festivities that were ongoing throughout the year. It was a yearlong joyous and happy occasion.

But now we must look forward to the challenges of the future for Union County, Kentucky. Challenges I know will be met and successfully overcome as the people of Union County join together to make our county a prosperous one and a great place to live. A great place to work, own a business, farm, mine coal, and raise our children.

I salute you, Union County.

Jerry Manning, Chairman
Sesquicentennial and Bicentennial Celebrations